BUSINESS STRATEGY EDITION 4

JOHN LOK

Copyright © John Lok
All Rights Reserved.

This book has been published with all efforts taken to make the material error-free after the consent of the author. However, the author and the publisher do not assume and hereby disclaim any liability to any party for any loss, damage, or disruption caused by errors or omissions, whether such errors or omissions result from negligence, accident, or any other cause.

While every effort has been made to avoid any mistake or omission, this publication is being sold on the condition and understanding that neither the author nor the publishers or printers would be liable in any manner to any person by reason of any mistake or omission in this publication or for any action taken or omitted to be taken or advice rendered or accepted on the basis of this work. For any defect in printing or binding the publishers will be liable only to replace the defective copy by another copy of this work then available.

Table of content

Chapter 1 Strategy Theory

Q1 How reduces transport cost of shipping or road transportation to the most minimum level in warehouse, factory locations by linear programming management science solution method ? p.3-20
Q2 How applying inventory Models Management Science Solution Method to solve factory transport cost challenge ?
Q3 How does Mathematical programming management science solve the Transportation Problem to cholocate retail stores case ?
Q4 Waiting Line Queueing Models management science solves public transport passenger queue problem ?
Q5 How to appl management games model solves salespeople emotion problem in store environment ?
Q6 How to apply management science classical theory solves internet invention to raise smart phone sale number increases ?
Q7 How to apply GAME THOERY SOLVE IBM AND MICROSOFT COMPUTER LARGE COMPANIES COOPERATION MANAGEMENT PROBLEM CASE ?
Q8 How to apply New trade game theory to bring IBM and Micro software both compaines cooperative advantages ?
Q9 How to apply Management Science Dependency Theory to raise Macrosoft and IBM software cooperational success ?
Q10 Can applying management technoloigcal science method to solve Society's Problems, artificial intelligence, computer, mobile, big data digial internet etc. high technological methods?

Chapter 2 Organizational Behavioral Theory
Q1 How to apply robotic to raise efficiency and productivity and improving performance for manufacture as well as bringing long term productive economic benefit to manufacturers? p.21-39

Q2 How to apply knowledge manamgement to improve organizaional behavior?

Q3 How do you feel about having diverse teams present in the modern workplace?
Q4 What Information Technology Outsourcing brings organizational advantages ?

Q5 How can Outsourcing or insourcing in human resource bring organizational advantages?

Q6 What are the disadvantages of local contracting to organizations?

Q7 How can global outsourcing source strategy to bring a value supply chain advantages to organizations?

Q8 How to motivate outsourcing, evidence of what is being outsourced risk and concerns to impact organizational behavioral change ?

Q9 How does environmental uncertainty factor influence organizational behavioral change ?

Q10 Can outsourcing bring what benefit of work skills to organizations ?

Q11 How future organizational skill needs how to change to bring positive workforce advantages to employees ?

Q12 What are regional dynamic skills influence global any organizational labour market demand ?

Chapter 3 Economy Theory

Q1 What is time series perspective on economic growth to pursue for growth and human development strategies ? p.40-55

Q2 How to apply quantitative evidence to review policy to improve economic growth ?

Q3 How individual tax payable honest behavior influences economic growth ?

Q4 How does every country government teach its citizen to do social moral honest behavior which can brings economic growth?

Q5 How can natural environment protection policy influence economy growth ?

Q6 How financial crisis influences economy growth ?

Q7 Can national leadership and economic growth has close relationship? Can leader individual behavior affect economic growth?

Q8 Why do future labours need to learn worldwide readiness skills ?

Q9 Why does future global skillful labor soft knowledge skill need increase ?

Contents

Preface   *vii*

1. Strategy Theory   1

2. Organizational Behavioral Theory   32

3. Economy Theory   64

Preface

Introduction

In our business society, we are facing different kinds of business challenges in different countries business environment. However, in any organizations, staffs and employers also encounter different department difficulties, if we do not know how to find solutions or implement effective strategies to solve these organizational challenges. Our organizations will not achieve raise efficiencies or improve performance. So, if we can predict any kinds of challenges which will be possible to occur as well as we can know how to implement effective strategies to solve these problems. Consequently, we may avoid any challenges occur to cause our organizational failures.

In my this book, I shall attempt to give some opinions to solve any kinds of orgnizational challenges. I shall indicate any business environment challenge and explain the most effective strategies to attempt to solve these challenges. Readers can understand how and why that this kind of strategy which is the most effective solution to this organizational challenge in this organization.

Strategy Theory

Q1 How reduces transport cost of shipping or road transportation to the most minimum level in warehouse, factory locations by linear programming management science solution method ?

linear programming management science solution method :

Researching the main shipping or /and road transport problem to bring cost rising to between either warehouse or/ and factory or both and the goods transfer transport destinations.

Inventory Models management science method helps warehouse, factory locations to reduce road or shipping transporation cost between goods transfer locations. For certain types of inventory control problems, certain models that attempt to minimize the cost associated with ordering and carrying inventories have been developed.

Transportation problem is a particular class of linear programming, which is associated with day-to-day activities in our real life and mainly deals with logistics. It helps in solving problems on distribution and transportation of resources from one place to another. The goods are transported from a set of sources (e.g., factory) to a set of destinations (e.g., warehouse) to meet the specific requirements. In other words, transportation problems deal with the transportation of a single product manufactured at different plants (supply origins) to a number of different warehouses (demand destinations). The objective is to satisfy the demand at destinations from the supply constraints at the minimum transportation cost possible. To achieve this objective, we must know the quantity of available supplies and the quantities demanded. In addition, we must also know the location, to find the cost of transporting one unit of commodity from the place of origin to the destination. The model is useful for making strategic decisions involved in selecting optimum transportation routes so as to allocate the production of various plants to several warehouses or distribution centers.

Suppose there are more than one centers, called 'origins' , from where the goods need to be transported to more than one places called 'destinations' and the costs of transporting or shipping from each of the origin to each of the destination being different and known. The problem is to transport the goods from various origins to different destinations in such a manner that the cost of shipping or transportation is minimum. Thus, the transportation problem is to transport various amounts of a single homogenous commodity, which are initially stored at various origins, to different destinations in such a way that the transportation cost is minimum.

Q2 How applying inventory Models Management Science Solution Method to solve factory transport cost challenge ?

A tyre manufacturing concern has many factories located in many different cities transport cost case

For certain types of inventory control problems, certain models that attempt to minimize the cost associated with ordering and carrying inventories have been developed. The objective of the transportation model is to determine the amount to be shipped from each source to each destination so as to maintain the supply and demand requirements at the lowest transportation cost.

For example: A tyre manufacturing concern has many factories located in many different cities. The total supply potential of manufactured product is absorbed by retail dealers in different cities of a country. Then, transportation problem is to determine the transportation schedule that minimizes the total cost of transporting tyres from various factory locations to various retail dealers.

The transportation model can also be used in making location decisions. The model helps in locating a new facility, a manufacturing plant or an office when two or more number of locations is under consideration. The total transportation cost, distribution cost or shipping cost and production costs are to be minimized by applying the model. How do you calculate the cheapest way to ship goods between several warehouses and stores? In this lesson, you will explore the transportation problem and its solutions.

Q3 How does Mathematical programming management science solve the Transportation Problem to cholocate retail stores case ?

Mathematical Programming Management Science Solution Method:

It attempts to maximize the attainment level of one goal subject to a set of requirements and limitations. It has extensive use in business, economics, engineering, the military and public service, mainly as an aid to the solution of allocation problems.

Imagine yourself owning a small network of chocolate retail stores. To run a successful business, you will also have to own or rent a warehouse where you will store the goods ready to be delivered whenever the stores need them. If you have only one warehouse, it will be supplying all your stores. However, as soon as you expand and open a second warehouse, you will have to make an important decision: which warehouse will deliver which goods to each of your stores? Depending on the choice you make, you might save or spend a significant amount of money.

The transportation problem is a distribution-type problem, the main goal of which is to decide how to transfer goods from various sending locations (also known as origins) to various receiving locations (also known as destinations) with minimal costs or maximum profit. As long as the number of origins and destinations is low, this is a relatively easy decision. But as the numbers grow, this becomes a complicated linear programming problem. Think about Walmart. In 2016, it had 5,229 stores and 166 distribution centers in the US! It would be impossible to calculate the optimal shipping routes without a computer algorithm.

General transportion problem types

Transportation problems can be classified into different groups based on their main objective and origin supply versus destination demand. Transportation problems whose main objective is to minimize the cost of shipping goods are called minimizing. An alternative objective is to maximize the profit of shipping goods, in which case the problems are called maximizing.

In a case where the supply of goods available for shipping at the origins is equal to the demand for goods at the destinations, the transportation problem is called balanced. In a case where the quantities are different, the problem is unbalanced.

When a transportation problem is unbalanced, a dummy variable is used to even out demand and supply. A dummy variable is simply a fictional warehouse or store. For example, if total supply at all warehouses is 50 units, but total demand at all stores is only 40 units, we create a fictional store with an additional demand of 10 units. The cost of shipping to the fictional store is usually zero. Now, the transportation problem becomes balanced. It is worth noting that sometimes problems that are solved using the transportation method have nothing to do with an actual movement of goods. What is crucial for applying the method is to recognize the network of connected elements.

Q4 Waiting Line Queueing Models management science solves public transport passenger queue problem ?

Waiting Line (Queuing) Models: solution imbalanced taxi and passenger queue in urban public transportation service case

The Four Problems Of Urban Transportation (And The Four Solutions)

The fixed-route bus and the bicycle solve at least one urban problem better than new technologies urban transportation problem case. There are four main problems in urban transportation that require four separate solutions. Some urban transportation design recommendion argued that technology can solve some problems, but not the same problem that public transit solves."The city has four separate problems of urban transportation which have four separate kinds of solutions, and it is very important to not mistake the solution for one problem for the solution for a different problem."

The first solution :

Bus stop time real -time information technology and apps solution method

Friction arises between a transit system and its users when the users don't have the information they need when they need it. That problem has been largely solved, Walker said, by information technology and apps. "That has been a fantastic transformation. Some of you may not be old enough to remember what life was like without real-time information, when you just went right out into the snow and wondered when the bus was coming."

The second solution:

Innovation method

The innovation method solves the city has four separate problems of urban transportation may include: Emissions and Energy Efficiency: "for which we're currently working on electric vehicles, and that's fantastic." Labor and

Safety: The cost of labor is the primary driver of operation costs for passenger transport, Walker said. "It is why your bus doesn't come more often, and it is also why Uber can't make money." Autonomous vehicles will address that and the accident rate. "There is a problem with the efficient use of labor, and also a colossal problem of safety for which we are talking about autonomous vehicles, and that's fantastic." Space: "And there is a fourth problem which is the efficient use of space, for which the solution is on the one hand, cycling and walking, and on the other, public transit provided by big vehicles."

The third soution:

The fixed-route bus or train solutione method is the best solution reason

The fixed-route bus or train is the vehicle of the future, because it remains the most efficient way to move large numbers of people through the congested space of a city. In his critique of public transit, Musk pointed out that people prefer "individualized transport, that goes where you want, when you want," like the Tesla Model S. But Walker contends individualized transport that goes where you want when you want can't move people through a congested city as efficiently as a fixed-route bus.

"We are always going to need vehicles sized to the appropriate capacity requirement, which means big buses in big cities," he said. "Our friends in the tech industry, including many of you here, and I love what you're doing, are always trying to sell us stories about how everything will fit together into a magnificent fusion. They want us to mix it up, to think about how it combines. And I'm always saying, but wait a minute, if you're going to be a smart customer you have to think about how they work separately as well."

Instead of above technological methods to solve public transport problem. The queue control management method will be one good solution

How do I conduct queue management of passengers in waiting taxi or bus area for Public transportation Vehicles?

Are there existing design projects and studies that a public transportation vehicle (Taxi or Bus) would know the number of passenger in waiting area/shed through long range network? I am conducting a design project for buses in my country that would know the number of passenger in waiting area and this information will be sent to the terminal or bus which will they used to pick up these passengers. Thus, congestion of buses and passenger can be lessen

I think that there are 2 technical issues: a) how to collect and transmit information, b) how to manage public transportation to minimize queue. About the 1st question you probably need either to do it manually (operator sitting at every station and making phone calls like "please send one more bus urgently, we have 100 of people waiting here", but this may be too expensive, at least for city buses) or to do it automatically (video camera, some image recognizing software that calculates people and then sends a message to the center) in this city has four separate problems of urban transportation concerns taxi and bus queue case.

Conclusion of the best solution method

As I know, there is not such a system design yet. but you may devise one by using the queue theory and optimizing the performance of the system by the following pattern:

- defining a objective function corresponding to the total passengers awaiting time.

- optimizing the objective function by finding the best set of assigning the available buses to the stations (considering the routes)

Waiting Line (Queuing) Models: solution imbalanced taxi and passenger queue in airport case

Predicting Imbalanced Taxi and Passenger Queue Contexts in Airport management problem

For certain types of problems involving queues, special descriptive models have been developed to predict the performance of service systems such as car garages – cars standing in queue for servicing.

The taxi and passenger queue contexts indicate the various states of queues related to taxis and passengers (i.e. taxis are waiting for passengers, passengers are waiting for taxis, both are waiting for each other, none is waiting). Predicting these queue contexts in a future time is very important for better airport ground transport operations. However, queue context prediction at the airport is a challenging problem due to the presence of different contextual factors i.e., time, weather, taxi trips, flight arrivals and many more. Also these taxi and passenger queue contexts at the airport are imbalanced since some of the contexts are very infrequently occurring compared to others. In this paper, we address the problem of predicting imbalanced taxi and passenger queue contexts at the airport. First, we investigate different contextual factors, including time, taxi trips, passengers and weather for queue context prediction. Then we propose a detailed step by step solution to address this problem. To support the effectiveness of our detailed approach, we generate a queue context dataset by fusing three real world datasets including taxi trip, passenger wait time and weather condition that represent the taxi and passenger queue contexts at any major international airport in any country City. The experimental results demonstrate that our developed queue context prediction framework provides detailed solutions to deliver higher accuracy in queue context prediction.

Therefore, context-aware mobility analytics enables the provision of intelligent analysis on mobility contexts considering different user perspec- tives. The success of many applications such as transport management and location recom- mendation requires the discovery of valuable knowledge through extensive analysis of related factors . For example, an airport can be regarded as the first and last impression of a city. Since a longer passenger wait time for a taxi ride can diminish the satisfaction rating of an airport , the authorities try hard to maintain a higher customer satisfaction rating by providing various mobility services such as easy and comfortable airport transfer to the city using taxicabs. However, the demand-supply equilibrium of taxis is highly dependent on the taxi drivers' decisions to make airport trips. The ubiquitous data can help with managing the mobility of airport users by detecting different mobility contexts (i.e. situa- tions of the concurrent queues related to passengers and taxis) . The intelligent analysis and prediction of different mobility contexts can help with making mobility decisions for airport passengers and taxis at different times of the day.

We argue that by incorporating the temporal deviation of taxi drivers' moves as the feature importance score can identify good quality neighborhoods and thus significantly boost the taxi-passenger queue context prediction accuracy. We utilize a real world queue context data set that includes information from taxi trip logs, airport passenger arrivals and weather conditions which are relevant to the different queue contexts. Then we propose a temporal driver-knowledge deviation based feature importance scheme to select a quality neighborhood for predicting taxi and passenger queue contexts.

As we extract more features by computing the deviations of all feature values from its hourly mean along with the current features of the queue context dataset , it is necessary to check the relevancy of all features. The reason is that the use of all these features may degrade the prediction performance significantly due to the inclusion of some irrelevant and redundant features. Also, for different stations, the configurations such as lane numbers, and maximum queue length of taxis and passengers can affect the solution of the passenger-taxi queue problem.

The proliferation of pervasive devices in smart cities has enabled the development of many smart mobility applications . Smart parking is one of the innovations that provides easy to use parking services to the urban commuters by leveraging pervasive sensors and flexible payment systems.

Inferring a situational awareness map using clustering methods has become a popular research topic in recent years. GPS trajectory has been utilised in smart mobility applications. In this section, we briefly review the related work which can be separated into two categories: points clustering and trajectory clustering. For example, intelligent reminders of user activities and notifications for major transporta- tion delays due to the current situation of the users. This outcome can also be leveraged for the applications of discovering user rou- tines based on personal contexts of mobile users. In an intelligent healthcare scenario, a robust and simultaneous recogni- tion of multiple user contexts would be important to be considered for elderly and disabled people, while travelling through various accessible paths .

Q5 How to appl management games model solves salespeople emotion problem in store environment ?

Any organizations can let salespeople feel happy to sell their products. Then their sale performance will also raise. The question concerns that how to make them to feel happy to help the organization to sell their products? I shall explain how to apply managment games or management psychological methods to solve this organizational problem as below:

How to manage sales for predictable revenue?

In order to hold salespeople sale psychology whether they feel happy or unhappy, executives need to understand the essential activities, sales managers must focus on to be analysts for change, foster continuous improvement and create a sales culture that drives results. Sale executives need to know how to achieve top objectives of sales management is to drive sales, capture new revenue and exceed monthly sales and margin objectives, e.g. performing sale straregy development with each salesperson on Monday morning at a minimum, and in a formal one-on-one meeting during the week;using strategy tools and questioning techniques to ensure the prospects are qualified and the strategy is valid; knowing the ratio between future values and future monthly quotos to raise sale opportunities; six month on-going sale plan aims to make sure there are coordinated to achieve sale to various market segments; developing on ongoing series of networking events to build market awareness in order to ensure all salespeople attend specific events involved in networking by salespeople to, understanding the market how to influence salespeople sale method to sale number, understanding trends and seeking some channels to raise additional sales opportunities; how to create trained or warm sale environment to let sales teams feel happy to sell.

How to design and utilize efficient control sale procedures?

The sale cycle procedure may include these market activities, such as advertising, sales promotion, market research, physical distribution, pricing , sale place, sale staffs seeking. SO, any organizations need have good sale planning, direction and control of the personnel, selling activities of a business with including recruiting, selecting, training, rating, supervising, paying or reward system, motivating strategy , as all these tasks apply to the personnel sales-force.

The factors may influence salespeople psychology, they may include fair income reward system, or appreciation methods and sale career development plan to every salesperson. It aims to encourage them to achieve the highest sale effort. Anymore, methods to train sale managers have the right direction to guide, lead and motivate their salespeople, e.g. knowledge of salespeople psychology needs how to satisfy them, understanding why they choose to do or act themselves sale behaviors in order to improve their weakness to motivate salespeople to achieve company's sale target goal every month easily, e.g. raising profitability, sales volume, market share, growth and corporate image building raise clients' confidence to choose to buy this company's any products more easily.

The sales organization is required for the following purposes, they may include: enabling top-management, to devote to more time in policy making for the growth and expansion of business to divide and fix authority among the subordinates , so that they may shirk work, to avoid repetition of duties and functions, so that there may not be any confusion among them to locate responsibility of each and every employee , so that they can complete the whole work in stipulated time, if not then the particular person must be responsible, to establish the sales effort to enforce proper supervision of sales force.

What does the concept of salespeople replacement value mean?

What is a sales force turnover management tool?

Sales force turnover is defined as the rate at which salespeople leave an organizations, resignations, retirements or dismissals. So, if the organization can raise the sales force turnover ratio, because many salespeople can be promoted or the retirement, or the sales force turnover ratio raising reasons as well as they are not resignation or dismissal reasons. I believe that the organization ought have good sale environment and reasonable reward and welfare strategy to let its salespeople feel happy to help this company to sell its products every day.

However, sales management's actions have direct or indirect effects to impact on turnover. Direct effects may include the firm's firing or dismiss policy. The indirect effects on sale turnover may include new salesperon recruiting and selecting policies affect the quality and performance of the sale force as well as the speed at which salespeople are replaced. The same policies have an impact on the sales force turnover rate through the characteristics of the newly recurited salespersons and the promotion , training, retraining policies, support, supervision, compensation. ALl of those factors have an impact on salesperson's personal satisfaction or dissatisfaction absolutely. So, any sale organizations need to concern how and why whether any one of above these factors may influence their salespeople how to perform or act sale behaviors in order to excite their sale number more effective in long term.

How to achieve sale force management effectively?

Sale management is one strategy to many organizations, because organizations expect their salespeople can only raise product sale number. So , they will consider whetther how to implement the sale management strategy to be the most suitable to themselves sale organizations in order to excite their sale teams to sell their products to achieve sale growth aim effectively. So for organization's long term sale growth development, it seems that one excellent sale management strategy can help the organization has stable sale number growth in long term possible.

However, the term " selling" includes a variety of sales situations and activities. For example, those sales positions where the sales representative is required primarily to deliver the product to the customer on a regular or periodic basis. The emphasis is this type of sales activity is very different to the sales position where the sales representative is dealing with sales of capital equipment to industrial purchasers. IN additions some sales representatives deal only in export markets whereas others sell direct to customers in their homes. So, sale organizations need to sell to local or overseas market as well as its target customer is businessmen or individual consumer or both in order to implement to choose their most suitable sale management strategy to train their salespeople more effective or achieving sale growth objective only. Because these its sale major target and where sale market place both factors will influence how it ought train its salespeople, so any organization's training method ought be influenced to change by whom is its major sale target and where is its major sale market location factors.

How to know the psychology of salesmanship?

When the organization can predict or find reasons to explain why its salespeople feel unhappy to help this organization to sell its products. Then, it can attempt to improve its weaknesses in order to let its salespeople to feel more sale service satisfactory feeling to continue to help this organization to sell its products. Then, it won't need not often to train or recruit new salespeople to replace its old salespeople in consequence.

How to know what its salespeoples' real need in order to raise their sale service satisfactory feeling ?

Psychology means that " science of the mind" and psychology plays to important part in business and it is quite worth to bring to influence any organization salespeoples' posivitive or negative sale emotion in their every sale process between themselves and their every client in personal. For example, if the salesperson often have negative emotion or he feels unhappy in every sale process, then he will encounter or increase many times of sale failure possibilities. He will feel that he is one poor verbal advertiser or seller or promotor to help his organization to promote its products to sell again as well as he will lose confidence to sell any products next sale chance, because his failure sale experiences are accumulated to influence his sale emotion to be poor or difficult sale.

Hence, the poor performance salesperson needs have more successful sale experiences to compensate his / her prior many sale failure times feeling, if the organization hopes this poor performance salesperson can raise sale number easily. Overall, any organizations need to concern how to improve or raise the more failure times of sale experience salespeoples' sale techniques or methods or attitudes more than choose to fire or dismiss them as well as finding another new salesperson to replace him/her. Because it is possible that the salesperson's poor sale performance that is not due to himself/herself poor sale effort and sale knowledge or lacking sale experience to the product, it may be due to the poor sale team cooperation relationship , feeling poor or not comfortable sale physcial shop environment, poor sale manager and other salespeople working relationship, the sale manager lacks leadership effort, poor family relationship etc. external factors more than himself/herself personal poor or negative emotion or poor health etc. personal factors. Hence, the organization ought enquire him/her why he/she feels unhappy to sell its products and it needs to attempt to find methods to solve his/her challenges immediately. If his/her challenges can be solved. It is possible that his/her sale efforts can be also raised for. So, if the organization can know how to utilize positive sale emotion psychological methods to predict or know why and how every salesperson perform his/her sale behavior in whose daily sale tasks, then it can concentrate on implementing effective and the most suitable sale training to raise their sale abilities more easily.

However, the sale training may include: How to build or improve long term good salesperson and his/her customer sale service relationship between every salesperson and every client in every buying and selling cycle process, how to using right communicating styleds for better understanding every client's real needs, powers and negotiating, e.g. every salesperson needs to review why there are many clients do not choose to buy any products from his sale presentation or promotion, finding every time sale failure reasons can let the salesperson makes himself/herself sale failure reasons evaluation or judgement in order to find what is the major reason influences his/her sale failure, e.g. lacking product knowledge, he/she often let many clients to feel that he lacks patience to listen the client's enquiry or feedback, his sale presentation is not attractive to let many clients like to stay longer time to listen his sale presentation in whole sale process, the salesperson himself/herself emotion is negative and he /she can let many clients feel he / she is not happy or does not enjoy to sell this product from himself/herself face impression or sale behavior impression easily, lacking enough sale techniques to persuade his/her clients why he/ she ought choose to buy this product in whole sale process etc. these factors may influence the salesperson's sale failure chance to be raised. Hence sales manager ought need to spend long time to meet the poor sale performance salesperson to discuess what his/her sale challenges are the most major to influence his/her every sale successful chance in order to improve his/ her sale performance more successfully.

In conclusion, the reasons why salespeople often encounter sale failure possibilities. The factors may include these aspects, such as they lask the desire to help customers to make satisfactory purchase decisons, they only concern how to achieve sale final objective or aim only, it will cause clients feel they do not real concern their real needs. They only concern to sell the product in success. They do not know how to describe the product whether what characteristics or features it owns accurately in order to increase sale chance to persudade them to make final decision to by the product, they do not attempt to participate the whole sale process to help them to choose the most right product in order to satisfy their any purcahse needs, they ought avoid deceptive or manipulative influence tactics, avoid the use of high pressure sales techniques etc. Thus, if any organizations can spend time to investigate what factors cause why any one of salespeople choose perform his/her sale behavior often in order to know or understand their salespeople' sale psychology absolutely. Then, I believe that their sale number will only grown more easily.

Q6 How to apply management science classical theory solves internet invention to raise smart phone sale number increases ?

Why does internet can influence smart mobile phone consumers' purchase desire? Has internet have direct relationship to influence smart mobile phone buyers' purchase desires ? Can the smart mobile phone talking product still attract phone buyers' preference choice, if it lacks internet function? Can internet raise smart phone sale number and create many mobile phone inventors and manufacturer occupations to raise GDP real GDP when smart phone buyers number and smart phone related occupation needs increase. I shall apply behavioral economic theory to attempt to explain the reasons how and why internet has direct relationship to influence smart mobile buyers' preference talking product choice in this traditional home telephone talking product market as below:

Is the internet putting up a barrier between people, even in bed? Does internet influence mobile phone consumers have not choose to buy because they are influenced to use mobiles when they use mobile to link internet to see any movies, or phones or news and influence their sleeping time in habit and they won't have nervous to work or learn on day time. We compulsively carry our smartphones with us wherever we go. The classroom, the bathroom, the bedroom, the outdoors — our phone is always in hand as if it were some magic self-defense tool capable of protecting us from all that is evil in the world. It all happened so fast. We didn't have the time to set any boundaries for smartphone usage, and now we find ourselves unable to save our relationships and form meaningful interactions with those dear to us.Smartphones are very useful in many circumstances. However, although not ruining your relationships per se, they can harm it in devious ways.

A smartphone is a modern day distraction that is so common, it's hardly noticed any more. It accompanies us wherever we go, demanding our attention multiple times a day. A phone call, a Facebook notification. We become irrevocably immersed in our digital lives, prioritizing the virtual world over anything else. Is it really that important to Instagram your dinner, rather than actually savoring it and sharing your impressions – or maybe a forkful of the dish – with the person next to you?Smartphones get in the way of our relationships, making it impossible for us to wholeheartedly devote our attention to the present moment. As a result, we lose many moments of wonder that are unique and never to be lived again.

Addiction to smartphone usage is a common problem among adults worldwide. It manifests itself in the excessive usage of their phones, while engaged in other activities such as studying, driving, social gatherings and even sleeping. However, many people fail to realize that addiction to smartphone usage is a serious issue that can have a negative effect on the person's thoughts, behavior, tendencies, feelings, and sense of well-being. In particular, it can be a risk factor for depression, loneliness, anxiety and sleep disturbances. As per the Mental Health Foundation in the United

Kingdom, people with depression experience an unhappy mood, loss of interest or pleasure, feelings of guilt or low self-worth, disturbed sleep or appetite, low energy, and poor concentration. Depressive and anxiety disorders are two main common disorders that are highly prevalent globally, as over 300 million people are estimated to suffer from depression, which is equivalent to 4.4% of the world's population. It is speculated that not only addiction to smartphone usage can affect one's mental and behavioral status, but also that those with mood disorders are more likely to become addicted to using their smartphones .

Numerous tools have been utilized in literature to assess the same phenomenon, but with different terms such as excessive smart phone usage, smartphone addiction, dependency on smart phones, internet addiction, problematic mobile phone usage, and so on. Remarkably, there was a tendency to use a non-pathological terminology, such as "Problematic Smartphone Use," rather than the term smartphone addiction. Addiction manifests itself in various forms such as preoccupation, tolerance, lack of control, withdrawal, mood modification, conflict, lies, excessive use and loss of interest. Several studies have found that women are more likely to develop an addiction to smartphone usage than men. This was viewed as a positive way for people to stay connected in social relationships. One study clarified that women like to show affection to their families using their smartphones while men use phones for efficiency and practicality . Though there are several studies on this topic, no study has proven this connection so far. Smartphone addiction has been found to be correlated with various physical and psychological issues, as indicated in a number of studies that tested this relationship among various age groups. For example, one study found that people with depression, social anxiety and loneliness had different uses for their smartphones compared to others. People with social anxiety made fewer outgoing calls, as well as, fewer text messages than those without social anxiety. It was reported that high levels of smartphone addiction were correlated with low self-esteem, loneliness, depression and shyness.

Although, internet can bring smart mobile phone users to spend sleeping time to use this kind of mobile product to watch movies, watch TV, listen music, social media communication, searching etc. non-talking communication behaviors. It seems that internet may influence smart phone users to change their phone purchase choice to buy the kind common mobile product more. But, in behavioral economic view, internet can bring smart mobile phone product has more attractive strengths to influence common mobile phone kind product users to chooce to use smart mobile phone products in preference. Internet can also bring these positive emotion to persuade the common mobile users to choose to use them.

Convenient applying: Any smart phone users can apply smart phone to link to internet to replace home computers to link to internet to watch movies, watch TV, listen music, social media communication, searching etc. non-talking communication behaviors in anywhere and any time conveniently. It is one kind of small size and light talking communication tool, but it can also help any mobile users to apply smart phone product to apply internet to do the same computer tasks in any time and any places. Hence, smart mobile can bring many computer users to feel that they can apply computer to do similar internet search behaviors at home. Convenient internet search function is one attract function to influence traditional computer users to choose to apply smart phone tools to replace computers tools to apply internet to search information, news, watch TV, movie, lisen music etc. social media communication behaviors at homes. When they bring smart phone to any where, then they can apply this tool to click to internet to do the same computer and internet link tasks in order to enjoy their entertainment needs. So, they do not need to apply computer tool to link to internet to enjoy their visal entertainment at homes. They can bring smart phone to go to anywhere to link to internet to enjoy their visal entertainment in any time conveniently. So, smart phone can be replaced to home computer tool to solve any visal entertainment enjoyers' needs.

● Internet brings smart phone users to feel more visal entertainment enjoyment

The Internet has revolutionized direct communication, lead to the digitization of books and film, as well as made convenience even more important. Companies have developed strategies that capitalize on the growing desire for easily accessible goods and services in only a few mouse clicks. As technology grows increasingly local and more connected to all aspects of the customer purchasing process, small business owners need to be more efficient in how they target their markets. Understanding why convenience plays such a large role in the purchasing process is vital in growing a successful business. Here are five trends that have popped up in recent years as businesses looked for ways to help their customers take advantage of well-timed opportunities. Internet can bring more attract to smart phone users, instead of visal enjoyment needs, the reasons may include as below:

1. Prior Consumer Knowledge

In today's digital world, consumers are looking for retail solutions which allow them to maximize their free-time and to stretch their disposable income. Due to this economic climate, small businesses which are able to provide their customer with a more convenient experience than a large retailer, are cashing in. H.M Cole, a custom clothier, offers its customers an entire planned wardrobe for the upcoming year after an hour's consultation. Other convenience services such as Trunk Club and Stitch Fix, personalized styling sites for men and women respectively, take that one step further in creating a complete look. These levels of convenience take a simple fitting and turn it into a way for consumers to spend less time deciding outfits, and more time doing other things they value.

2. Direct-to Store Delivery

Due to the "larger-than-life" nature of big box stores, they have begun to develop strategies which combat the convenience of a smaller retailer. The newest trend among these chains is to offer direct-to store delivery. Shoppers are able to find what they are looking for online, and purchase directly on the site. Rather than having to wait the 3-5 days for delivery, chains are making their purchases available (sometimes at discounted rates) for pick up at their local store. Essentially, customers are taking part in shopping services where the store physically groups together the inventory, saving the individual time in their purchases.

3. Personalized Billing, Shipping Info

Customer profiles across frequently visited webpages allow for consumers to not only keep their billing information in one place, but also have access to similar products or content. Businesses are able to not only track purchases, but to specifically target an individual with the information provided for convenience sake. A user does not usually choose to re-enter billing or shipping information on a site they frequent, and so by saving this information, a company is removing an obstacle that might otherwise influence the purchase.

4. Time is Money

Fast food and drive-thru options have changed the world's nutritional demands, creating a society of cheap convenience foods. Although the nutritional value of these highly-processed foods is lacking, the demand for them has been on the rise across the globe. While these types of businesses are growing at a record rate, the pressure to remain affordable and convenient has driven them online.
Some innovative restaurant chains have transitioned to online ordering which provide an easy, personalized interface for their customers to select and buy all from the website portal. A restaurant receives the order digitally, packages the food, and then sends it out to delivery, often for an additional fee. Both Google and Amazon , as well as many startups, have launched services that deliver meals and groceries to your home. Time has shown that customers are willing to spend a little more for the convenience of having food arrive at their doorstep.

5. Subscription Services

Another recent convenience service trend is through subscription services. This can include streaming goods such as TV shows, movies, audio books, or music tracks. Companies charge their customers a fee to have access to a database of content whenever, wherever they want. Some providers have included commercials as a means to generate more income. Other subscription services include coffee of the month clubs, or deliver gift boxes. These companies charge a monthly (or yearly) subscription fee and compile a box of themed goodies for their customers.While some very big companies have struggled to make convenience a larger part of their customers' experiences, many small businesses that offer niche products and services have an advantage in this area. The Internet is helping them to level the playing field in a way. It provides a platform for small businesses to capitalize on the demand for goods by using convenience to win fans and new customers.
On conclusion, internet can bring smart phone users to do any activities when they need to apply computer tools at home in any time and anywhere. So, internet has direct relationship to persuade mobile phone or computer users to choose to buy mobiles for communication uses or internet uses in preference nowadays as well as internet can bring the different kinds of new or unique mobile phones design needs increase to achieve the creating mobile phone inventors and mobile phone manufacturers occupations necd. So, it seems that internet can influence mobile phone product's occupations needs and mobile phone consumers number increase to raise real GDP growth to the smart

phone maufacturing and sale country really.

Reference

Bigne, Enrique (2005). The impact of internet user shopping patterns and demographics on consumer mobile buying.

Falk, Louis, K. et. al (2005) " E-commerce and consumer's expectations: What makes a website work". Journal of website promotion, 1(1), 65-75.

Parasuraman, A., Zeithaml, V.A. and Berry L.L. (1988) SERVQUAL: A multiple-item scale for measuring consumer perceptions of service quality. Journal of retailing, 64, 12-40.

Q7 How to apply GAME THOERY SOLVE IBM AND MICROSOFT COMPUTER LARGE COMPANIES COOPERATION MANAGEMENT PROBLEM CASE ?

Economics is just as much about consumer and producer behavior as it is about finance or the allocation of resources. With that in mind, game theory will explain one of the most fundamental tools economists use to frame competitive decision making. It provides a systematic approach to decision-making in competitive environments and a framework for the study of conflict.

Game theory solves the Prisoner's social criminal behaviors

Two small-time criminals are out breaking into cars, stealing what they can. They are working together in the same area of town. Fortunately, they get caught and booked down at the station. The detective goes in to question them separately and offers them both the same deal: they can either confess or stay silent. Their punishment will be determined by what action they take and what action the other perp takes. Here's what could happen:

a) If both perps confess, they each get 3 years.

b) If both perps stay silent, they each get 1 year.

c) If perp #1 stays silent and perp #2 confesses, perp #2 serves NO time and perp #1 serves 10 years.

d) If perp #2 stays silent and perp #1 confesses, perp #1 serves NO time and perp #2 serves 10 years.

So, if you were perp #1, what would you do? You could stay quiet and count on only getting one year, hoping that your friend stays quiet as well, and you'll both only serve 1 year. But, what if you admit to being involved and they admit being involved as well, then you'll both get 3 years. Or, what if you stay silent but your friend admits? Then you'll get 10 years; that wouldn't be good! Well, it is if your friend stays quiet.

The lesson to be learned from the prisoner's dilemma described above is how difficult it is to make an optimal decision when two competitors - and that's what these two perps are right now - can't collaborate. Typically, the economic man (or woman) is someone who makes decisions based on their own self-interest and chooses that which maximizes their own benefits. The entire idea behind game theory is that the result of your decision isn't known to you until you find out what your friend (or competitor) is going to do, so you have to make the best decision you can based on the information you have.

Game Theory in Real Life

We know how game theory works in a fictional situation that would never really happen, but what about how game theory applies to real life? Well, we can talk about that, too. Think about any strategic decision a business might make. The success or failure of that decision may very well depend on how the competition reacts. Perhaps a fast food restaurant wants to build a new location on the corner of a popular intersection. They complete their analysis of traffic flow, demand, other options in the area, etc., and ultimately decide it's a good idea. Then, once construction begins, another restaurant opens up a new location across the street, with a new building plan that includes drive-through ordering. What does our first restaurant do now?

Technology marketing cooperative strategy

Future when the thinking capabilities of computers approach our own is quickly coming into view. Raid process in coming decades will bring about machines with human –level intelligence capable of speech and reasoning, with a myriad of contributions to economics, politics and warcraft. The birth of true artificial intelligence will profoundly affect humankind's future. In our future technological development market, what it will bring much influences to economy. I shall indicate these several aspects, they may include as below:

On artificial intelligent invention brings high unemployment to low skill employees aspect, from the time the last artificial intelligence break through was reached in the last 1940s, scientists around the world have looked for ways of this " artificial intelligence" to improve technology, raising efficiency and productivity beyond what even the most sophisticated of today's artificial intelligence programs can achieve. Even now, research is ongoing to better understand what the new AI programs will be able to do, when remaining within the intelligence such as human brain. Most AI programs currently programmed have been limited primarily to making simple decisions or performing simple operations on relatively small amounts of data.

AI technological invention will bring much contribution to influence our future economic development. It had unique characteristics to compare common machines and it can help many industries to raise efficiency, productivity and improve performance as well as consumer individual self use. Such as the network is not taught to understand prose in any human sense. Instead, during its training phase, it adjusts the internal connections in its simulated neural networks to best anticipate the next word. It can be applied to read any article and understand any meaning to write any article as same to authors' mind and writing ability. For example, in the future, any one entered the first few sentences of any article, you are reading, the algorithm spewed out two paragraphs that sounded liked a freshman's effort to recall the gist of an introductory lecture on machine learning during which she was daydreaming. The output contains all the right words and phrases , not bad. So, (AI) technology can be applied to become just one more example of programs that do things thought to be uniquely human playing the real-time strategy game, translating text, making personal recommendations for books and movies, recognizing people in images and videos. But with the invention, of deep neural networks and the massive computational of the tech industry, computers improved until their outputs to longer appeared . In the future, algorithms can best humans, (AI) can help human to do any things in possible. Then, our society will encounter one automobile machine working environment. Does (AI) innovation will low skill employees lose their jobs because robotic can replace to any human to do simple jobs in any industries. Whether machines can become sentient matters for ethical reasons. If computers experience life through their own senses, they cease to be purely a means to an end determined by their usefulness to us humans. Then our society will have many jobs which are needed to be worked by human, due to (AI) or robotic invention, it can replace human to do many simple jobs, e.g. factory manufacturing jobs, warehouse deliver jobs, public transportation , e.g. tram, train, ferry, underground train, bus etc. driving tasks, they are replaced by robotic auto driving, even pilot flying job will be also replaced to drive air planes by (AI) driving on sky impossible. Although, (AI) can help businesses to raise efficiency, increase productivity and improve performance, but it also bring these jobs to be replaced by (AI) and it will cause many people lose jobs when (AI) is invented to be applied in popular in our future societies. On business benefits aspect, (AI) can bring working efficiency and productivity improvement, but it can also bring unemployment ratio raises as the same time when employers accept to apply (AI) to replace human to any simple or difficult tasks.

So, we need to limit or prohibit (AI) invention to exceed human's extent in possible. I mean that we do not need to limit to invent any (AI) skill, but we need to concern human need to work in the same time. If (AI) was real replaced to do any simple jobs in any industries, then there are many low skill workers , such as factory workers, clean workers, drivers ,even high skill workers, such as lawyer, teacher, pilot. They will lose their jobs in possible. So, how to invent (AI) technology will influence our future global employment chance to provide us to continue to work in any organizations. So, (AI) will may bring high unemployment ratio, if it is applied to any low skill , even high skill jobs aspects to different industries in global.

On conclusion , in economist view, technology market development must need, such as (AI) invention because it can help any industries to raise efficiency, productivity and improve performance, but we need to know how it can be applied to avoid human to lose jobs, due to (AI) is replaced to do their tasks for any industries in possible. Whether (AI) invention can create jobs or bring job lose? (AI) scientists must need to consider how to invent their skill to be applied to which tasks aspect if they hope human won't lose many jobs to do in future one day.

Q8 How to apply New trade game theory to bring IBM and Micro software both compaines cooperative advantages ? New trade theory (NTT) suggests that a critical factor in determining international patterns of trade are the very substantial economies of scale and network effects that can occur in key industries.

These economies of scale and network effects can be so significant that they outweigh the more traditional theory of comparative advantage. In some industries, two countries may have no discernible differences in opportunity cost at a particular point in time. But, if one country specialises in a particular industry then it may gain economies of scale and other network benefits from its specialisation.

Another element of new trade theory is that firms who have the advantage of being an early entrant can become a dominant firm in the market. This is because the first firms gain substantial economies of scale meaning that new firms can't compete against the incumbent firms. This means that in these global industries with very large economies of scale, there is likely to be limited competition, with the market dominated by early firms who entered, leading to a form of monopolistic competition.

Monopolistic competition is an important element of New Trade Theory, it suggests that firms are often competing on branding, quality and not just simple price. It explains why countries can both export and import designer clothes. This means that the most lucrative industries are often dominated in capital-intensive countries, who were the first to develop these industries. Therefore, being the first firm to reach industrial maturity gives a very strong competitive advantage. (some may say unfair advantage)

New trade theory also becomes a factor in explaining the growth of globalisation. It means that poorer, developing economies may struggle to ever develop certain industries because they lag too far behind the economies of scale enjoyed in the developed world. This is not due to any intrinsic comparative advantage, but more the economies of scale the developed firms already have.

Examples of New Trade Theory

•Specialisation of IT in Silicon Valley – the US. Hewlett and Packard started their computer business. Success attracted more IT firms to that area. Not because of any particular intrinsic benefit but new firms start to get the network benefits of being around other IT setups.'

•Globalisation has led to increased variety for consumers. The proliferation of brand clothing labels. Firms competing in the model of monopolistic competition and heavy branding. Neither UK or Italy has a particular comparative advantage in producing clothes, but consumers are attracted to brand image of Italian and British fashion labels.

Moral hazard influences to Macrosoft or Microcorp and IBM software cooperational success problem

Moral hazard is when one party can take risks knowing the other party will bear the consequences. It describes the risk present when two parties don't have the same information about actions that take place after an agreement is in place. The situation creates a temptation to ignore the moral implications of a decision: doing what benefits you most instead of doing what is right.

Example of Moral Hazard in Insurance

Moral hazard is a term that originated in the insurance industry and spread to the financial sphere. To illustrate the concept, imagine you rent a car and opt for the maximum insurance coverage possible. Damaging the vehicle does not have significant negative consequences for you, because the insurance company pays for repairs—or a replacement car—if something happens.

The insurance company uses statistics to estimate how likely the vehicle is to suffer damage, and they price their services accordingly. You pay much less for insurance than it would cost to repair a car because, in most cases, the insurance company won't have to pay for any repairs. But there are times when you might have an unfair information advantage over your insurance company. That's where moral hazard comes in.

You plan to drive into the mountains on rough, narrow roads. So, you get the most generous insurance coverage possible, and you don't worry about bouncing over rocks or scratching the paint in thick brush along the side of the road. You might even have a perfectly good car available at home, but there's no way you're going to drive your vehicle up that road—so you rent a car and buy insurance. The low cost of insurance means you have no incentive to protect the car you rented, but the insurance company doesn't know you're driving it under such conditions.

Moral hazard happens when you have an incentive to take risks that somebody else will pay for. You get to do whatever brings you the greatest potential benefit, and you don't suffer the consequences. In this example, the insurance company bears the risk: the cost of repairing or even replacing the car. The more insulated you are from risk, the more temptation you face.

Examples of Moral Hazard in Lending

Moral hazard became a significant factor during (and after) the financial crisis that began in 2007. The concept can apply to both lenders and borrowers.

Lenders were eager to approve loans before the mortgage crisis. Some mortgage brokers encouraged "subprime" borrowers to lie on loan applications, or they altered documents to make it appear that borrowers were able to afford loans that they really couldn't afford. For example, sometimes they reported inaccurate income numbers or the brokers did not require documentation that would demonstrate a borrower's ability to repay the loan.

Why would lenders hand out money when they don't know if the borrower can afford the payments—especially if they have to commit fraud to get the loans approved? In many cases, the lenders were only originating, or selling, the loans. After approving and funding loans, lenders would sell the loans to investors, who eventually suffered the losses. In other words, the lender took little or no risk. But lenders had an incentive to keep making new loans because that's how originators generate revenue.

When things turned sour, lawmakers and the public got scared. They worried that if major banks collapsed (some of them were loan originators, while others held risky investments), they would bring down the U.S. economy—not to mention the global economy. Because these banks were considered "too big to fail," the U.S. government provided funding to help some of them to weather the economic storm. If those banks suffered significant losses, the government promised to protect deposits (in some cases through the FDIC). Of course, taxpayers fund the U.S. government, so the taxpayers were ultimately bailing out the banks. The moral hazard was the lenders and investment banks taking risks that had consequences not for themselves, but for taxpayers and others.

Borrowers

Moral hazard can occur in almost any agreement, whether it's an informal understanding or a formal contract. If one party has the opportunity to benefit from taking "risks"—while risking almost nothing—moral hazard is at play.

During the financial crisis, as millions of homeowners struggled to pay their mortgages and loan defaults skyrocketed, government programs offered relief. People could avoid foreclosure thanks to money and guarantees from the U.S. government.

The moral hazard in these cases was that borrowers, increasingly underwater on their home loans, would be tempted to walk away from their mortgage rather than repay it. Such an action would put risk back onto the lender. The hazard is that the borrower no longer had an incentive to do the right thing—to pay back the mortgage as agreed.

Hence, such as moral hazard applies to Macrosoft or Microcorp and IBM software cooperational case . If Macrosoft and Microsorp and IBM do not decide to co-operate to help themselves to expand their software strengths to achieve the aim to improve their software quality and feature and function, then they can not bring any software innovation to let future software users to raise any new softwares invention or improvement useful benefits. Then, global software market can not be improved to let any software users to raise high techological software products choices number. Because they are competitors, they won't hope themselves softwares' quality, feature and function and improvement are worse to compare other softwares companies among them. So, global software users will have moral hazard to enjoy any kinds of new softwares products invention in short time. But, if they can cooperate to buy and sell themselves both shares, then they both will be another softwares owners, they won't hope the another software company loses many software customers because itself new software inventions to attack the another software company. They must hope themselves any new software invention products , they can still attract many new software products customers together. Then, global software users won't have moral hazard to enjoy any new software invention products in short time, because they must cooperate to help themselve to improve their any new softwares ' qualities , features and functions in order to they can have many software customers share in these software market when they are global large software firms.

What are Principal-Agent Problems to Microsoft and IBM both large computer companies cooperation?

For example, a company's stock investors, as part-owners, are principals who rely on the company's chief executive officer (CEO), as their agent, to carry out a strategy in their best interests. That is, they want the stock to increase in price or pay a dividend, or both. If the CEO opts instead to plow all the profits into expansion or pay big bonuses to managers, the principals may feel they have been let down by their agent. There are a number of remedies for the principal-agent problem, and many of them involve clarifying expectations and monitoring results. The principal is generally the only party who can or will correct the problem.

Understanding the Principal-Agent Problem

The principal-agent problem has become a standard factor in political science and economics. The theory was developed in the 1970s by Michael Jensen of Harvard Business School and William Meckling of the University of Rochester. In a paper published in 1976, they outlined a theory of an ownership structure designed to avoid what they defined as agency cost and its cause, which they identified as the separation of ownership and control.The trend has been towards contracts with the agent that link compensation directly to performance measurements set by the principal.

This separation of control occurs when a principal hires an agent, The principal delegates a degree of control and the right to make decisions to the agent. But the principal retains ownership of the assets and the liability for any losses.

Factoring in Agency Costs

Logically, the principal cannot constantly monitor the agent's actions. The risk that the agent will shirk a responsibility, make a poor decision, or otherwise act in a way that is contrary to the principal's best interest, can be defined as agency costs. Additional agency costs can be incurred while dealing with problems that arise from an agent's actions. Agency costs are viewed as a part of transaction costs.

Agency costs may also include the expenses of setting up financial or other incentives to encourage the agent to act in a particular way. Principals are willing to bear these additional costs as long as the expected increase in the return on the investment from hiring the agent is greater than the cost of hiring the agent, including the agency costs.

Examples of the Principal-Agent Problem

The principal-agent problem can crop up in many day-to-day situations beyond the financial world. A client who hires a lawyer may worry that the lawyer will wrack up more billable hours than are necessary. A homeowner may disapprove of the City Council's use of taxpayer funds. A home buyer may suspect that a realtor is more interested in a commission than in the buyer's concerns. In all of these cases, the principal has little choice in the matter. An agent is necessary to get the job done.However, there are ways to resolve the principal-agent problem.

Solutions to the Principal-Agent Problem

The onus is on the principal to create incentives for the agent to act as the principal wants. Consider the first example, the relationship between shareholders and a CEO. The shareholders can take action before and after hiring a manager to overcome some risk. First, they can write the manager's contract in a way that aligns the incentives of the manager with the incentives of the shareholders. The principals can require the agent to regularly report results to them. They can hire outside monitors or auditors to track information. In the worst case, they can replace the manager.

Contract Clauses

In recent years, the trend has been towards employment contracts that connect compensation as closely as possible with performance measurements. For managers of businesses, incentives include performance-based awards of stock or stock options, profit-sharing plans, or directly linking management pay to stock price. At its root, it's the same principle as tipping for good service. Theoretically, tipping aligns the interests of the customer, or the principal, and the agent, or the waiter. Their priorities are now aligned and are focused on good service.

Hence, such as this IBM and microsoft large both companies, if they hope to cooperate , they need to solve which company can have more management authority and which company can have more share owming or investing authory. If IBM can have more management authority to control their both companies, but IBM has less shares number to Microsoft, e.g. IBM has 30 % shares to Microsoft, whether IBM ought earn more profit or less profit to 30% profits from Microsoft, if IBM have more management authory, but IBM can not cooperate to Microsoft to assist it to raise more computer buyers number. So, agent problem will cause IBM and Microsoft cooperation more easily together in nowadays computer market. But, if IBM can help Microsoft to increase computer buyers number after IBM participates to manage Microsoft's internal organizational management , then IBM can increase Microsoft computer buyers number in long time. Then, their cooperation can be more success, it means that their principle and agent problem will solve between them.

Q9 How to apply Management Science Dependency Theory to raise Macrosoft and IBM software cooperational success ?

● Macrosoft or Microcorp and IBM software cooperational strategy

What is information technologic game strategy? How and why information technological game strategy can influence economic growth? I shall explain as below:

Nowadays, Macrosoft and Microcorp are the global information technological big companies. They own much market share in global information technological industry. Whether what factors influence they can still be global information technological products leaders. Why does computer software consumers still choose their products to compare other software products in preference? I suppose that Macrosoft and Microcorp, their hypothetical any software games have developed a clever new computer game that is certain to be very popular. Although Microcorp have the unique competitive advantage with its own software game engineers and compete against Macrosoft, but it can so it cheaper and better if it can hire any Macrosoft's software game engineers. So, in economic view, it needs to pay high salary (higher cost) to hire Macrosoft's engineers (labor), but Macrosoft's engineers can help Microcorp to invent any new kinds of software games to compete Macrosoft. Although, Microsorp needs to pay higher labor cost, but when it can raise its any software games' design and game playing methods to attract any game players. Then, these new and exciting software games can help it can bring many game entertainment players and then it can sell cheaper price to raise more attractive effort to win its competitor (Macrosoft). So, higher software game designing engineers (skill labor), their game designing effort will be the major factor to influence any one information technological companies in success. If one software designing company can employ one high software game designing effort profession to help it to design any kinds of attractive software games. Although, it may pay high salary (labor cost), but it have much chance to attract many software game buyers to compare that if it pays less salary to employ one poor game software designing profession. Because the poor software game designing profession may need to spend long time to research how to design any kinds of attractive game software to excite game players' playing desires in this playing software game industry market. Long time research to the poor software game designer may be one none any reward to compensate to the software game designing firm when it needs to pay long time salary to employ him. Otherwise, if the software game designing firm can accept to pay higher salary to the higher software game designer, he will have higher chance to help it to design any more attractive software games to influence game players' playing game entertainment desires. So, any software game designing companies their game designers (labor) must be the major factor to influence their business succeeds or fails in this software game entertainment market.

On the employing method hand, Microcorp can choose to include in its contracts with its software engineers that from working for another Macrosoft software company for a certain period of time if they resign from Macrosoft. A move such as this is sometimes called a preeptive move. Its propose is to alter its rivals' payoffs in order to alter their employing strategies. Preemptive moves are usually costly (high slaary), and this one is no exception. In its employment contracts makes Macrosoft a less attractive to let its old game software engineers want to leave their current employer, such as Macrosoft. As a result, Macrosoft must pay its software game designing engineers above the going market salary if it hopes their employment contracts can be continue between Macrosoft and its software game engineers.

Should Macrosoft must need to decide how to react. It can choose to fight Microcorp by aggressively advertising its game, which is costly high, but gives it a larger market share in the game player entertainment market, when Macrosoft had any one profession game software engineer(s) leave(s) his company and he/they change(s) to the another Microcorp software game designing company to work, or it can forego the expense of an advertisement campaign and simply share the market 50/50 with its major competitor, Microcorp to be partners.

Their competition has close relationship to influence economic growth because it will have many game players number to be increase if they can cooperate to be partners in success when they can design any new kinds of software game products to satisfy software game players' entertainment feeling. Otherwise, if they can not be one good partners and they only consider their every business benefits and neglect themselves business benefits. Then, their software playing games sale price can either to be reduced in order to attract any software game players when their software games can not be designed to have much new playing methods to attract many game players. Consequently, the GDP income to this software game entertainment market must reduce because any kinds of entertainment software games prices are reduced as well as the game players number is also decreasing. Due to they are the major software entertainment game suppliers in global. Any game players will only choose either Microcorp or Macrosoft to buy their any kinds of entertainment software game products to play majorly. So, their software game manufacturing and sale number must influence global GDP income increases or decreases in macro economy view. It implies that any countries technological software game industry's GDP income will depend on these both Microcorp and Macrosoft software game's cooperation relationship whether they have good or bad cooperation relationship. If their cooperation relationship is good, then they can manufacture high quality and attractive entertainment software games as well as raising sale price and exciting many game players' entertainment desires to achieve the increase to game players number aim more easily.

How to achieve their cooperation relationship more easier. I suppose that, in the software game entertainment industry, over its lifetime, the computer game will generate $500,000 in new income (income minus production cost) for all the firms producing it or its clones. Macrosoft must pay its software engineers an additional $100,000 to get them to agree to accept a contract containing an anticompetition clause. It costs Microcorp $100,000 to develop the software if it can hire Macrosoft's engineers and $200,000 otherwise. Aggressive advertising costs Macrosoft $70,000 and has the effect of giving it a 80% market share if it restricts its engineers' employment and a 72% market share if it does not. So, the fall in total market share is caused by the fact that without some of Macrosoft's advertisements. If however, Macrosoft passively acquiesces to Microcorp's entry and shares the market, then both firms can still achieve a 50% market share fairly. Hence, they must need to achieve 50/50 market share if they hope to achieve the cooperation relationship in success. Otherwise, they will not achieve cooperation relationship in success. However, the spending advertisement factor will also their cooperation chance in success. For example, it would be more realistic to recast the Software Game as one in which Macrosoft chooses how much to spend on advertising with sales depending continuously on the amount spent. Other examples of continuous cooperation choices may include: the productive capacity of an electrical power plant; the salary to offer a prospective employee; or the insurance premium to charge a prospective policyholder. So, the amount to any of these expenditure factor will influence whether they will decide to cooperate to sell their software games products in global game entertainment market.

How and why Macrosoft and Microcorp's cooperation can influence global economic growth? It is significant that Macrosoft and Microcorp both technological software game designing companies are global the largest firms, they are doing international software game trade business to many countries and they have large market share in the software entertainment game sale market. Aside from trade based on technological gaps and software game product cycles, software game entertainment industry is dynamic in nature or game players' entertainment taste will change any time in completely static in nature. That is, given the nation's game players' playing taste and game entertainment factor, such as game playing designing technological method and game player individual playing game taste both. We proceeded to determine the nation's comparative advantage and the gains from the different kinds of entertainment software game designing supply factor and the game player individual game taste changing factor. So, any nation's software game players number will depend on these both factors to influence whether their number will either increase or decrease in the year in this global software game entertainment market. However, these factors can be changed by time, technology usually can improve any software game playing methods and game player individual playing taste will also change any time. As a result, the nation's comparative advantage also changes over time, such as when the nation has many game players lose their interest to buy any software games to play, then the nation ought not only consider how to develop its software entertainment game in the technological industry, it is right time to research any other new technological industries to develop if it still hopes its GDP income can rise in the technological industry overall aspect. Such as dynamic trade theory is still in its infancy. However, our comparative statics analysis can carry us a long way in analyzing the effect on international trade resulting from changes in factor technology, and tastes over time, such as entertainment software game case.

The growth of factors of production will also influence the software game entertainment industry development, through time, a nation's population usually grows and with its size of its labor force , such as China and India. Similarly, by utilizing part of its resources to produce capital equipment, e.g. India needs to utilize its technological resources, technological engineers and technological material can need to be used to manufacture either new software game products or computers. But, its technological resources will be shortage (both labor and technological material). So, many technological companies choose to apply more technological material and technological engineers to use much time and money to manufacture any new software game products. Then, these labor and material resources will be reduced to be spent time and material to manufacture any new computer products in the year. In this technological industry case, capital refers to all the man-made means of production, such as machinery, factories, communication and education and training of labor force, all of which greatly enhance the nation's ability to produce either computer products or software game products. So, the national will also continue to assume that it can experiencing economic growth is producing two commodities, such as software game and computer both kinds of technological products under the constant returns to scale. So, if India can not raise the rapid technical process to skill labor and supply technological material supplying number to satisfy to manufacture the enough software game and computer products to supply them to sell to any countries' playing game players and computer users every month. Then, its technological industry will lose many clients, due to it can not supply enough software games and computers number to sell to any countries.

Several empirical studies have indicated that most the increase in real per capita income in technological industrial nations is due to technical progress and much less to capital accumulation. However, the analysis of technical progress is much more complex than the analysis of factor growth because there are several definitions and types of technical progress, and they can take place at different rates in the production of either or both commodities, such as software game and computer.

Technical progress is usually classified into neutral, labor saving , or capital saving. All technical progress , regardless of its types reduces the amount of both labor and capital required to produce any given level of output. So, if India could have good technical progress to raise its technological labor skill and reducing the technological material to be used to manufacture the software games and computers. Then, it will have chance to keep the maximum manufacturing level number to software game and computer products as the same time.

Q10 Can applying management technoloigcal science method to solve Society's Problems, artificial intelligence, computer, mobile, big data digial internet etc. high technological methods?

Updated with recent issues such as the national debate on health care reform, this Second Edition of How Can We Solve Our Social Problems? Social problems, also called social issues, affect every society, great and small. Even in relatively isolated, sparsely populated areas, a group will encounter social problems. Part of this is due to the fact that any members of a society living close enough together will have conflicts. It's virtually impossible to avoid them, and even people who live together in the same house don't always get along seamlessly. On the whole though, when social problems are mentioned they tend to refer to the problems that affect people living together in a society.

The list of social problems is huge and not identical from area to area. In the US, some predominant social issues include the growing divide between rich and poor, domestic violence, unemployment, pollution, urban decay, racism and sexism, and many others. Sometimes social issues arise when people hold very different opinions about how to handle certain situations like unplanned pregnancy. While some people might view abortion as the solution to this problem, other members of the society remain strongly opposed to its use. In itself, strong disagreements on how to solve problems create divides in social groups.

Other issues that may be considered social problems aren't that common in the US and other industrialized countries, but they are huge problems in developing ones. The issues of massive poverty, food shortages, lack of basic hygiene, spread of incurable diseases, ethnic cleansing, and lack of education inhibits the development of society. Moreover, these problems are related to each other and it can seem hard to address one without addressing all of them.

It would be easy to assume that a social problem only affects the people whom it directly touches, but this is not the case. Easy spread of disease for instance may tamper with the society at large, and it's easy to see how this has operated in certain areas of Africa. The spread of AIDs for instance has created more social problems because it is costly, it is a danger to all members of society, and it leaves many children without parents. HIV/AIDs isn't a single problem but a complex cause of numerous ones. Similarly, unemployment in America doesn't just affect those unemployed but affects the whole economy.

It's also important to understand that social problems within a society affect its interaction with other societies, which may lead to global problems or issues. How another nation deals with the problems of a developing nation may affect its relationship with that nation and the rest of the world for years to come. Though the United States was a strong supporter of the need to develop a Jewish State in Israel, its support has come at a cost of its relationship with many Arabic nations.

Additionally, countries that allow multiple political parties and free expression of speech have yet another issue when it comes to tackling some of the problems that plague its society. This is diversity of solutions, which may mean that the country cannot commit to a single way to solve an issue, because there are too many ideas operating on how to solve it. Any proposed solution to something that affects society is likely to make some people unhappy, and this discontent can promote discord. On the other hand, in countries where the government operates independently of the people and where free speech or exchange of ideas is discouraged, there may not be enough ideas to solve issues, and governments may persist in trying to solve them in wrongheaded or ineffective ways. The very nature of social problems suggests that society itself is a problem. No country has perfected a society where all are happy and where no problems exist. Perhaps the individual nature of humans prevents this, and as many people state, perfection many not be an achievable goal.

On conclusion, social problem-solving might also be called 'problem-solving in real life'. In other words, it is a rather academic way of describing the systems and processes that we use to solve the problems that we encounter in our everyday lives. The word 'social' does not mean that it only applies to problems that we solve with other people, or, indeed, those that we feel are caused by others. The word is simply used to indicate the 'real life' nature of the problems, and the way that we approach them.

A Model of Social Problem-Solving

One of the main models used in academic studies of social problem-solving was put forward by a group led by Thomas D'Zurilla.

This model includes three basic concepts or elements:

•Problem-solving

This is defined as the process used by an individual, pair or group to find an effective solution for a particular problem. It is a self-directed process, meaning simply that the individual or group does not have anyone telling them what to do. Parts of this process include generating lots of possible solutions and selecting the best from among them.

•Problem

A problem is defined as any situation or task that needs some kind of a response if it is to be managed effectively, but to which no obvious response is available. The demands may be external, from the environment, or internal.

•Solution

A solution is a response or coping mechanism which is specific to the problem or situation. It is the outcome of the problem-solving process.

Once a solution has been identified, it must then be implemented. D'Zurilla's model distinguishes between problem-solving (the process that identifies a solution) and solution implementation (the process of putting that solution into practice), and notes that the skills required for the two are not necessarily the same. It also distinguishes between two parts of the problem-solving process: problem orientation and actual problem-solving.

Problem Orientation

Problem orientation is the way that people approach problems, and how they set them into the context of their existing knowledge and ways of looking at the world. Each of us will see problems in a different way, depending on our experience and skills, and this orientation is key to working out which skills we will need to use to solve the problem.

An Example of Orientation

Most people, on seeing a spout of water coming from a loose joint between a tap and a pipe, will probably reach first for a cloth to put round the joint to catch the water, and then a phone, employing their research skills to find a plumber. A plumber, however, or someone with some experience of plumbing, is more likely to reach for tools to mend the joint and fix the leak. It's all a question of orientation.

Problem-solving includes four key skills:

1.Defining the problem,

2.Coming up with alternative solutions,

3.Making a decision about which solution to use, and

4.Implementing that solution.

Based on this split between orientation and problem-solving, D'Zurilla and colleagues defined two scales to measure both abilities.

They defined two orientation dimensions, positive and negative, and three problem-solving styles, rational, impulsive/careless and avoidance.

They noted that people who were good at orientation were not necessarily good at problem-solving and vice versa, although the two might also go together.

It will probably be obvious from these descriptions that the researchers viewed positive orientation and rational problem-solving as functional behaviours, and defined all the others as dysfunctional, leading to psychological distress.

The skills required for positive problem orientation are:

Being able to see problems as 'challenges', or opportunities to gain something, rather than insurmountable difficulties at which it is only possible to fail. Believing that problems are solvable. While this, too, may be considered an aspect of mindset, it is also important to use techniques of Positive Thinking; Believing that you personally are able to solve problems successfully, which is at least in part an aspect of self-confidence. Understanding that solving problems successfully will take time and effort, which may require a certain amount of resilience; and motivating yourself to solve problems immediately, rather than putting them off.

Those who find it harder to develop positive problem orientation tend to view problems as insurmountable obstacles, or a threat to their well-being, doubt their own abilities to solve problems, and become frustrated or upset when they encounter problems.

The skills required for rational problem-solving include:

a. The ability to gather information and facts, through research. There is more about this on our page on defining and identifying problems;

b. The ability to set suitable problem-solving goals. You may find our page on personal goal-setting helpful;

c. The application of rational thinking to generate possible solutions. You may find some of the ideas on our Creative Thinking page helpful, as well as those on investigating ideas and solutions;

d. Good decision-making skills to decide which solution is best. See our page on Decision-Making for more; and

e. Implementation skills, which include the ability to plan, organise and do. You may find our pages on Action Planning, Project Management and Solution Implementation helpful.

Potential Difficulties

Those who struggle to manage rational problem-solving tend to either:

a. Rush things without thinking them through properly (the impulsive/careless approach), or

b. Avoid them through procrastination, ignoring the problem, or trying to persuade someone else to solve the problem (the avoidance mode).

c. This 'avoidance' is not the same as actively and appropriately delegating to someone with the necessary skills (see our page on Delegation Skills for more). Instead, it is simple 'buck-passing', usually characterised by a lack of selection of anyone with the appropriate skills, and/or an attempt to avoid responsibility for the problem.

An Academic Term for a Human Process?

You may be thinking that social problem-solving, and the model described here, sounds like an academic attempt to define very normal human processes. This is probably not an unreasonable summary. However, breaking a complex process down in this way not only helps academics to study it, but also helps us to develop our skills in a more targeted way. By considering each element of the process separately, we can focus on those that we find most difficult: maximum 'bang for your buck', as it were.

How Technology Can Help Solve Societal Problems

What Are Science and Technology?

Science and technology have completely changed the world over the last 200 years. Human life expectancy has doubled. We've learned how to communicate and travel rapidly across the entire globe. We're surrounded by televisions, computers, electric lights, cars, cell phones, and all kinds of things that would have been unimaginable even a century ago. And none of it would be possible without science and technology.

Science is the systematic study of the natural world, through observation and experiment. Technology is the use of scientific knowledge for practical purposes, to complete tasks that wouldn't be possible without it. Technology can be super simple, like the wheel, or super complicated, like the personal computer. Either way, we are surrounded by it in our modern lives.

Can applying management technoloigcal science method to solve Society's Problems, artificial intelligence, computer, mobile, big data digial internet etc. high technological methods?

Sometimes it might seem like technology only causes problems or complicates things. People yearn for a simpler life, without cell phones beeping, traffic jams, and dangerous weapons. But the truth is, science and technology have solved a lot of society's problems and will continue to do so in the future.

However, nowadays, human is encountering " The Network Revolution" stage. And so is it today. The Fourth Industrial Revolution — what Klaus Schwab (founder of the World Economic Forum) defines as the fusion of technologies blurring the lines among the physical, digital and biological spheres — is upon us. Meanwhile, nationalism is colliding with globalism, machine learning and artificial intelligence advancing geometrically, and global warming is on a direct path to changing the very nature of our planet. Despite these many challenges, this revolution, like the many that have preceded it, also comes with a great promise of opportunity.

To be sure, there are reasons for great optimism. In just the past 30 years, the global poverty rate halved with many of the poorest people in the world becoming significantly less poor. These gains mirror dramatic improvements in health and education including advances in life expectancy, child mortality, health care provision, among other important areas. Moreover, most of these gains predate the effective integration of digital technologies into the cause. In short, it is reasonable to argue that the potential for social 'changemakers' armed with today's digital platforms in partnership with large and growing virtual networks can dramatically improve the human condition.

Some management scientists beleive that "The potential for social 'changemakers' armed with today's digital platforms in partnership with large and growing virtual networks can dramatically improve the human condition."

I shall indicate how " Self-organization Powered by Technology" technological management scinece method , it can be applied to help any organizations, even our societies to solve many organizational or social problems nowadays.

What is our nowadays Civil society ? What are the differences or changes between our traditional civil society and nowadays civil society? How and why does technological innovation influence our civil social change, e.g. internet, ecommerce, smart phone ?— the network of institutions that define us as actors in the civil sphere independent of governments — is supposed to serve as the leader in promoting pluralism and social benefit. As Klaus Schwab notes that "a renewed focus on the essential contribution of civil society to a resilient global system alongside government and business has emerged." Unfortunately, nonprofit groups, academic institutions and philanthropic organizations engaged in social change are struggling to adapt to the new global, technological and virtual landscape.

This new direction starts with social organizations fundamentally rethinking the core assumptions driving their attitudes, behaviors and beliefs about creating long-term sustainable value for their constituencies in an exponentially networked world. Rather than using an organization-centric model, the nonprofit sector and related organizations need to adopt a mental model based on scaling relationships in a whole new way using today's technologies model.

Embracing social change as a platform is more than a theory of change, it is a theory of being — one that places a virtual network or individuals seeking social change at the center of everything and leverages today's digital platforms (such as social media, mobile, big data and machine learning) to facilitate stakeholders (contributors and consumers) to connect, collaborate, and interact with each other to exchange value among each other to effectuate exponential social change and impact.

Civil society is grounded in exploiting new digital technologies, but extends well beyond them to focus on how organizations think about advancing their core mission — do they go at it alone or do they collaborate as part of a network? Nowadays, many business organizations or public organizations require thinking and operating, in all things, as a network. It requires updating the core DNA that runs through social change organizations to put relationships in service of a cause at the center, not the institution. When implemented correctly, SCaaP will impact everything — from the way an organization allocates resources to how value is captured and measured to helping individuals achieve their full potential.

Digital Platforms Empower Social Change at Scale

To be sure, early adopters are already using technology to effectuate change at a pace and scale not previously available in the physical and digitally disconnected world. The marginal cost of delivery remains too high. But with today's technologies, with support from the board and management to make it happen, social change at scale is possible. Just as Apple chose a platform approach when launching their App Store, these organizations are enabling their partners and contributors to share and co-create in the value chain they co-inhabit. Each has moved beyond allowing supporters to donate and promote, toward sharing real value through stakeholders' talents and assets.

The future of social change as a platform is a world of connected platforms working to solve society's most pressing challenges more effectively as fast as possible. These platforms will supersede and encompass existing social change organizations. Those organizations that embrace social change as a platform will lead the way in helping to usher in this new era of connected social change platforms.

The core assets needed today to advance social change — ideas, individuals and institutions — continue to be the primary ingredients. What is changing and will continue to change, however, is the way these assets are assembled to deliver maximum social impact. Organizations can achieve SCAAP to the extent that those with a shared cause can gradually maximize shared capability (platforms) and minimize organization products. This represents a radical shift in approach.

Every organization relies on its information, capabilities and assets to be effective, but their networks are largely untapped or underutilized. Creating more value and scaling social impact requires the organizations' leaders to leverage their networks, tapping into new sources of value, both tangible and intangible. Value in the social impact supply chain will continue to come from new sources, for those who allow that to happen. Existing stakeholders in social change organizations will add value in new ways and new stakeholders will interact in new ways with the community's resources and assets via the platform. SCaaP will increasingly bring all those actors and sectors together.

Some management scienists indicated that "The future of social change as a platform is a world of connected platforms working to solve society's most pressing challenges more effectively as fast as possible."

How technological innovation impacts our social change?

Our future social change will be impacted to these several aspects:

Social change organizations that leverage their stakeholder's networks as well as their tangible (programs and services) and intangible (expertise and relationships) assets will gain these and other advantages from embracing the SCaaP business model.

•Decreases costs: Stakeholders willing to share their opinions, skills, relationships and even real assets for shared value to the cause, at a very low or near-zero cost, stretch an organization's very scarce resources. Moreover, reinventing the wheel each time social change products and services are created lead to duplication and waste.

•Deepens community engagement: Enabling meaningful ways for stakeholders to add value increases engagement and deepens understanding and strengthens these relationships. SCaaP enables anyone with a good idea to build innovative services that connect citizens to the cause of their choice, allowing citizens to more directly participate.

•Increases organizational flexibility and decreases risk: Operating as a network increases an organization's adaptability and speed. Work is more distributed and lends itself to self-organizing, which makes it highly responsive to changing needs. Allowing common functions to be implemented as shared utilities across social change organizations instead of replicating them in each silo also reduces risk.

•Enhances transparency and accountability: SCaaP fundamentally shifts the power dynamic within the social change community. Grant makers work with community stakeholders as peers, helping them achieve full potential as individuals and their organizations.

•Expands impact: Ultimately, scaling relationships lets an organization secure more value, which helps maximize social impact. As co-creating partners who have a vested interest in advancing a cause, stakeholders' incentive to add value is clear. The platform's success is their success.

How technological management science method of internet platform ,which can impact our social change as well as it can be the best technological management method to help our societies to solve many social problems

Social change as a platform is first and foremost a business strategy, a theory of change that needs to be integrated into every organization's five-year strategic plan. That effort begins by identifying how and where an organization can accelerate the transition to a network-model across the entire organization. Specifically, organizations must assess their business model and inventory network assets, and start to reallocate resources and capital to networks as well as develop network key performance indicators (KPIs).

•Choose the right platform. Platforms that embrace intelligence, speed, productivity, mobility, and connectivity empower social change organizations to take advantage of the most significant transformations taking place in enterprise software.

•Select the relationships to scale. Identify all the key stakeholders for advancing your mission and indicate which relationships are the most important to scale. Be sure to include existing and potential relationships, including other partners and organizations that can add value.

•Connect programs and services. Plot the organization's various offerings — programs and services offers to various stakeholders — and map how each contributes value to advance the relationships with different stakeholders.

•Convert the data into intelligence. A unified view of relationships and programs creates troves of data. Convert the data into useful, real-time intelligence integrated into the organization's processes in real-time.

•Drive one-to-one engagement. Real-time intelligence lets organizations engage more effectively with all.

•Track what matters. It's not just financial performance that matters, but also engagement, sentiment and co-creation. Create KPI's for each of these items and add them to daily performance reviews.

•Keep platforms, networks and intelligence at the center. Products and services are helpful, but in the final reckoning, it is the breadth and depth of the network that will create the scale of social change desired.

On conclusion, I believe that internet platform is the best technological management method to help our, the nonprofit world will have the potential to enact social change on a scale previously unimagined. It is time to take up the mantle because doing so can unlock the future potential of every human being because human can gather any useful data to attempt to compare which is the best in order to solve any social problems in the short time as well as internet platform, e.g. big data gathering method will still be the most accurate and the most rapid speed to help any management scientists to learn how to analyze and conclude the problem solution in the most useful way more than other high technological methods nowadays.

CHAPTER TWO

Organizational Behavioral Theory

Q1 How to apply robotic to raise efficiency and productivity and improving performance for manufacture as well as bringing long term productive economic benefit to manufacturers?

It is one good question. Can scientists only concentrate on researching artificial intelligent for raising productivity, efficiency and improving performance to businesses aspect, so neglecting on research other scientific researching aspects? Technological marketing economy is as a play between independent individual subjects. However, it has also become clear that the notion of play has to be interpreted within a different framework than that of classical functionalism. In mainstream classical economics, interaction or exchange is understood as the effect of the ends-means rationally of individuals. Smith's sympathy –based view of man and society avoids this functionalistic reduction of interaction and exchange. For example, the utilitarian or functional aspect of , the social process of producing and distributing wealth through free exchange, is in Smith's view on part of the value and belief system which people in ordered and prosperous societies employ to give sense and meaning to their experiences.

Hence, in our business society, technology can bring marketing economic change to be better. One free technology marketing economic society must have these advantages to bring to influence our living, such as below:

It interprets and explains improving social processes of producing and distributing to business, such as (AI) skill invention , it can help businesses to improve performance and efficiency and productivities for their manufacturing aim only, but (AI) ought not be applied to replace to do all low skill workers' jobs in any positions in any factories or warehouses. So, any employers ought not dismiss all workers and they are replaced by all robotics. They will need to consider overall economic benefit. I mean that avoiding low skill workers unemployment ratio raises. For example, one factory can still keep 50% workers and 50% robotics to cooperate to work together. Because some human workers can be such as assistants to do any simple tasks in factory every teams. Human workers can discover any errors to let manager to know in order to improve in their cooperation process with robotics. So, human workers and robotics cooperation , it is more efficient manufacturing method to compare any manufacturing process is needed to finish from robotics only in any future factory or warehouse working environment. So, robotics and human workers cooperation can bring the most efficient production and distribution benefits to future manufacturers in any factories or warehouses because human can help robotics to find any error in order to improve. Otherwise, if the factory or warehouse has only all robotics to work. Although, they may bring raising productivities or improving performance and efficiencies. But they can not know whether how to improve their errors or revises their every time productive performance to be better every day. SO, the most efficient manufacturing method is that human workers and robotics cooperate to work together in any factories or warehouses.

On innovation and information economic influence aspect, one of the most important topics in economics is the economics of information. Information includes things as varied as e-mail, and even the text book you are reading. Information is a very different kind of commodity from things like pizza and shoes because information is expensive to produce , but cheap to reproduce. Because of the unusual nature of information, it is subject to market failure, so we need to develop different kinds of public politics to regulate it, the law of " intellectual property".

We are encountering the essence of economic development is innovation and that monopolists are in fact of innovation in a capitalist economy. What does the economics of information mean ? Who do we need to develop information economy? Modern economics emphasizes the special problems involved in the economics of information. Information is a fundamentally different commodity from normal goods. Because information is costly to produce , but cheap to reproduce, markets in information are subject to serve market failures.

For the production of software program industry example, the windows software, developing this program took several years and cost Microsoft many money of dollars. You can purchase a legal copy for $5. The same phenomenon is at work in pharmaceutical, entertainment and other areas where much of the value of a good comes from the information it contains. In each of these areas, the research and development to software on the product may be an expensive process that takes years. But once, the information is recorded on paper, in a computer or on a compact disc, it can be reproduced and used by a second person essentially for free.

The inability of firms to capture the full monetary value of their invention is called inappropriability. Inventions are not fully appropriable because other firms may imitate an invention, in which case the other firms may derive some of the benefits of the inventive investments. Sometimes, imitators may drive down the price of the new product, in which case consumers would get some of the rewards. Information consumers can earn these benefits when the value of an invention to all consumers and producers is many times the appropriable private return to the inventor (the monetary value of the invention to the inventor).

However, information is expensive to produce but cheap to reproduce. To the extent the rewards to invention are inappropriable, we would expect private research and development to be underfunded, with the most significant underinvestment in basic research because that is the least appropriable kind of information. The inappropriability and high social return on research can lead most governments to subsidize basic research in the fields of health and science and to provide special incentives for other creative activities. Thus, special laws governing patents, copyrights, business and trade secrets and electronic media create intellectual property rights. The purpose is to give the owner special protection against the material's bcing copied and used by others without compensation to the owner or original creator.

On the Internet information economic market influence hand, inventions that improve communications are hardly limited to the modern age. But the rapid growth of electronic storage, access and transmission of information highlights of providing incentives for creating new information. Many new information technologies have large sunk costs but virtually zero marginal costs. With the low cost of electronic information systems like the internet, it is technologically possible to make the large amounts of information available to everyone, everywhere, at close to zero marginal cost. Perfect competition is nowadays different e-commerce internet information business competitive feature, and any e-commerce merchants can not survive here because a price equal to a zero marginal cost will yield zero revenues and therefore no viable firms.

Hence, the economics of the information economy highlights the conflict between efficiency and incentives. On the one hand, all information ,might be provided free of charge, e.g. free e-book download, e-song download e-movie download from internet. Free provisions of information looks economically efficient because the price would thereby be equal to the marginal cost, which is zero. But a zero price on intellectual property would destroy the profits and therefore reduce the incentives to produce new books from authors, movies and songs from creators would earn little rewards from their creative activity. But with the costs reproduction and transmission so much lower for electronic information than for traditional information, so the future any electronic publishing industry 's products, e.g. e-books, e-songs , e-music, e-movies prices will be lower than traditional paper books, pack of songs and movies price, either consumers go to shops to buy them or consumers pay visa card to enter websites to buy any e-books , songs, e-music , e-movies from internet channel. Then, it will cause these traditional publishing and entertainment industries' competition to be raised because these e-publishers or e-entertainment can reduce their price to sell from their websites when their costs are nearly to zero. Hence, information technology can raise competition to the traditional publishing and entertainment industries. The traditional paper book, music, movie business merchants need to any authors or creators to help them to create any unique movies, songs, paper books to sell from their shops and they need to ensure their authors or music , movie creators won't give these creative book, song, movie products to any e-music, e-publisher, e-movie merchants to sell from their websites absolutely.

On conclusion, information technology influence any music, publish, movie creative product competitive raising to the traditional paper book publishers, music or movie publishers when many book publishers or music or movie creators choose e-commerce to replace traditional shop visiting sale method. So ﹐ it is possible to influence overall publishing and music and movie creative industries will change to e-commence consumption model. Then the traditional book and music and movie visiting stores will disappear and the online websites to these merchants will increase and their price also will reduce in global e-publishing and e-creative product consumption environment. So, information technology will bring some traditional store visiting number decreases and online merchant e-store number increases and consumers can pay less price to buy these creative products from internet.

Q2 How to apply knowledge manamgement to improve organizaional behavior?

In management science view, any organizations or societies need to know why our organizations or societies need to apply any kinds of management science method to help our organizations or societies to solve some problems, even all problems when our organizations or societies are encountering any kinds of problems. I shall explain what management science means and how and why one effective management organization or management society will let its citizen or its staffs to bring more welfares or benefits in its organization or society.

One effective or efficient or successful organization or society , it has these characteristics in its organization or its society.

1.It helps in Achieving Group Goals - It arranges the factors of production, assembles and organizes the resources, integrates the resources in effective manner to achieve goals. It directs group efforts towards achievement of pre-determined goals. By defining objective of organization clearly there would be no wastage of time, money and effort. Management converts disorganized resources of men, machines, money etc. into useful enterprise. These resources are coordinated, directed and controlled in such a manner that enterprise work towards attainment of goals.

2.Optimum Utilization of Resources - Management utilizes all the physical & human resources productively. This leads to efficacy in management. Management provides maximum utilization of scarce resources by selecting its best possible alternate use in industry from out of various uses. It makes use of experts, professional and these services leads to use of their skills, knowledge, and proper utilization and avoids wastage. If employees and machines are producing its maximum there is no under employment of any resources.

3.Reduces Costs - It gets maximum results through minimum input by proper planning and by using minimum input & getting maximum output. Management uses physical, human and financial resources in such a manner which results in best combination. This helps in cost reduction.

4.Establishes Sound Organization - No overlapping of efforts (smooth and coordinated functions). To establish sound organizational structure is one of the objective of management which is in tune with objective of organization and for fulfillment of this, it establishes effective authority & responsibility relationship i.e. who is accountable to whom, who can give instructions to whom, who are superiors & who are subordinates. Management fills up various positions with right persons, having right skills, training and qualification. All jobs should be cleared to everyone.

5.Establishes Equilibrium - It enables the organization to survive in changing environment. It keeps in touch with the changing environment. With the change is external environment, the initial co-ordination of organization must be changed. So it adapts organization to changing demand of market / changing needs of societies. It is responsible for growth and survival of organization.

6.Essentials for Prosperity of Society - Efficient management leads to better economical production which helps in turn to increase the welfare of people. Good management makes a difficult task easier by avoiding wastage of scarce resource. It improves standard of living. It increases the profit which is beneficial to business and society will get maximum output at minimum cost by creating employment opportunities which generate income in hands. Organization comes with new products and researches beneficial for society.

Any organizations or our societies can attempt to apply any kinds of management science knowledge to solve our organizational or social problems, but if our organizations or societies apply the wrong management science method to attempt to help our societies or organizations to solve our any problems. Then, the kind of wrong management science method will not bring advantages to our organizations or societies , even it can bring extra disadvantages to our organizations or societies. So, how to choose the most suitable management science method to solve our organizational or social problem, it is very important consideration to ourselves, when we feel that we have need to find the most suitable management science method to solve the kind of social or organizational problem.

Management science solves organizational problems

One successful or efficient or effective organization or society ought have good knowledge management strategy

I shall explain what is knowledge management and knowledge management will bring what advantages or disadvantages to our organizations or societies. Management science is one kind of knowledge management, it can help any organizations or societies to solve any simple or complex problems. Knowledge management is a systematic approach to capturing and making use of a business' collective expertise to create value. The potential advantages of effective knowledge management are significant but, as with most processes, there are certain challenges to consider.However, althouh, Knowledge management ought help business growth, but it also bring disadvantage when our societies or organizations apply this knowledge management method to attempt to solve their problems, they may include:

● Advantages and disadvantages of knowledge management

Advantages of knowledge management. Some of the common benefits of knowledge management include:

I. improved organisational agility

II. better and faster decision making

III. quicker problem-solving

IV. increased rate of innovation

V. supported employee growth and development

VI. sharing of specialist expertise

VII. better communication

VIII. improved business processes

A good knowledge management system will make it easy to find and reuse relevant information and resources across your business.

I. create better products and services

II. develop better strategies

III. improve profitability

IV. reuse existing skills and expertise

V. increase operational efficiency and staff productivity

VI. recognise market trends early and gain an advantage over your rivals

VII. benchmark against your competitors

VIII. make the most of your collective intellectual capital

Resourceful collaboration will bring more views, diverse opinions and varied experiences to the process of decision-making, helping your business to make decisions based on collective knowledge and expertise.

● Disadvantages of knowledge management

The key to any successful knowledge management system is knowing its limitations. Some of the common challenges include:

I. finding ways to efficiently capture and record business knowledge

II. making information and resources easier to find

III. motivating people to share, reuse and apply knowledge consistently

IV. aligning knowledge management with the overall goals and business strategy

V. choosing and implementing knowledge management technology

VI. integrating knowledge management into existing processes and information systems

To overcome these challenges, before any organizations or our societies decide to apply knowledge management to solve our problems, we ought need to consider these issues.

I. develop clear processes to capture, record and share business knowledge

II. define the scope and objectives of any knowledge management initiatives

III. create a corporate culture of knowledge sharing between employees and management

IV. set clear goals and strategies to help you utilise the collective knowledge (otherwise, it will be of no use to your business)

V. consider budget, strategy and training needs for any new knowledge management system

VI. consider change management strategies for introducing new knowledge management practices

Strategic management in management science view

Instead of knowledge management, we also need to know how we choose the most suitable strategic management method in order to help our societies or our organizations to solve any social or organizational problems in success. Strategic Management is all about identification and description of the strategies that managers can carry so as to achieve better performance and a competitive advantage for their organization. An organization is said to have competitive advantage if its profitability is higher than the average profitability for all companies in its industry. Strategic management can also be defined as a bundle of decisions and acts which a manager undertakes and which decides the result of the firm's performance. The manager must have a thorough knowledge and analysis of the general and competitive organizational environment so as to take right decisions. They should conduct a SWOT Analysis (Strengths, Weaknesses, Opportunities, and Threats), i.e., they should make best possible utilization of strengths, minimize the organizational weaknesses, make use of arising opportunities from the business environment and shouldn't ignore the threats.

Strategic management is nothing but planning for both predictable as well as unfeasible contingencies. It is applicable to both small as well as large organizations as even the smallest organization face competition and, by formulating and implementing appropriate strategies, they can attain sustainable competitive advantage. It is a way in which strategists set the objectives and proceed about attaining them. It deals with making and implementing decisions about future direction of an organization. It helps us to identify the direction in which an organization is moving.

Strategic management is a continuous process that evaluates and controls the business and the industries in which an organization is involved; evaluates its competitors and sets goals and strategies to meet all existing and potential competitors; and then reevaluates strategies on a regular basis to determine how it has been implemented and whether it was successful or does it needs replacement.

Strategic Management gives a broader perspective to the employees of an organization and they can better understand how their job fits into the entire organizational plan and how it is co-related to other organizational members. It is nothing but the art of managing employees in a manner which maximizes the ability of achieving business objectives. The employees become more trustworthy, more committed and more satisfied as they can co-relate themselves very well with each organizational task. They can understand the reaction of environmental changes on the organization and the probable response of the organization with the help of strategic management. Thus the employees can judge the impact of such changes on their own job and can effectively face the changes. The managers and employees must do appropriate things in appropriate manner. They need to be both effective as well as efficient.

One of the major role of strategic management is to incorporate various functional areas of the organization completely, as well as, to ensure these functional areas harmonize and get together well. Another role of strategic management is to keep a continuous eye on the goals and objectives of the organization.

Following are the important concepts of Strategic Management, when you are your country's social leader or you are your organization's business leader, you need to consider these steps in your strategic management arrangement, such as below:

Strategy - Definition and Features
Components of a Strategy Statement
Strategic Management Process
Environmental Scanning
Strategy Formulation
Strategy Implementation
Strategy Formulation vs Implementation
Strategy Evaluation
Strategic Decisions
Business Policy
BCG Matrix
SWOT Analysis
Competitor Analysis

Porter's Five Forces Model

Strategic Leadership

Corporate Governance

Business Ethics

Core Competencies

Advantages and Disadvantages of Cooperative Society

In micro view, organizational management science aspect, one successful cooperative social organization can create innovation advantages to any organizations, such as when one organization can apply management science to let it become one successful cooperative social organization. Although, it seems that one cooperative society is one sucessful management organization, but it also has disadvantages when the organization becomes one successful cooperative social organization.

An cooperative social management organization's

Advantages:

1. Easy Formation:

Compared to the formation of a company, formation of a cooperative society is easy. Any ten adult persons can voluntarily form themselves into an association and get it registered with the Registrar of Co-operatives. Formation of a cooperative society also does not involve long and complicated legal formalities.

2. Limited Liability:

Like company form of ownership, the liability of members is limited to the extent of their capital in the cooperative societies.

3. Perpetual Existence:

A cooperative society has a separate legal entity. Hence, the death, insolvency, retirement, lunacy, etc., of the members do not affect the perpetual existence of a cooperative society.

4. Social Service:

The basic philosophy of cooperatives is self-help and mutual help. Thus, cooperatives foster fellow feeling among their members and inculcate moral values in them for a better living.

5. Open Membership:

The membership of cooperative societies is open to all irrespective of caste, colour, creed and economic status. There is no limit on maximum members.

6. Tax Advantage:

Unlike other three forms of business ownership, a cooperative society is exempted from income-tax and surcharge on its earnings up to a certain limit. Besides, it is also exempted from stamp duty and registration fee.

7. State Assistance:

Government has adopted cooperatives as an effective instrument of socio-economic change. Hence, the Government offers a number of grants, loans and financial assistance to the cooperative societies – to make their working more effective.

8. Democratic Management:

The management of cooperative society is entrusted to the managing committee duly elected by the members on the basis of 'one-member one -vote' irrespective of the number of shares held by them. The proxy is not allowed in cooperative societies. Thus, the management in cooperatives is democratic.

Disadvantages:

In spite of its numerous advantages, the cooperative also has some disadvantages which must be seriously considered before opting for this form of business ownership.

The important among the disadvantages are:

1. Lack of Secrecy:

A cooperative society has to submit its annual reports and accounts with the Registrar of Cooperative Societies. Hence, it becomes quite difficult for it to maintain secrecy of its business affairs.

2. Lack of Business Acumen:

The member of cooperative societies generally lack business acumen. When such members become the members of the Board of Directors, the affairs of the society are expectedly not conducted efficiently. These also cannot employ the professional managers because it is neither compatible with their avowed ends nor the limited resources allow for the same.

3. Lack of Interest:

The paid office-bearers of cooperative societies do not take interest in the functioning of societies due to the absence of profit motive. Business success requires sustained efforts over a period of time which, however, does not exist in many cooperatives. As a result, the cooperatives become inactive and come to a grinding halt.

4. Corruption:

In a way, lack of profit motive breeds fraud and corruption in management. This is reflected in misappropriations of funds by the officials for their personal gains.

5. Lack of Mutual Interest:

The success of a cooperative society depends upon its members' utmost trust to each other. However, all members are not found imbued with a spirit of co-operation. Absence of such spirit breeds mutual rivalries among the members. Influential members tend to dominate in the society's affairs.

Advantages and Disadvantages of Diversity in the Workplace

In micro organization view, management science can bring advantages of diversity in the workplace to the organization, but it also being disadvantages to the organization. They may include as below:

People like to stay in their comfort zones. That is why routines develop over time. When we feel safe, then the idea is that we can be more creative in every element of our life. This process envelopes our personal and professional lives. There are ways that we try to become comfortable at work on our own, like bringing a potted plant to the office or taping a favorite comic strip to the computer. About 2 out of every 5 employees also say that they love their job because of the presence of their co-workers. When there is a supportive team and supervisor in place, it is easier to pursue what we are passionate about as a career.

The issue with diversity is that it takes some people out of their comfort zone. Some professionals define the composition of the perfect team as people who come from the same culture, ethnicity, educational experience, or social status. If someone on the team has a different set of life experiences, then the unknowns that come about because of it can feel scary. When people are afraid, then their focus is on survival instead of productivity. Even though the pros and cons of diversity in the workplace show that teams can by over 30% more productive when they focus on uniqueness, some people are not ready to step outside of their comfort zone. They would rather trade short-term comfort for long-term profit losses.

Q3 How do you feel about having diverse teams present in the modern workplace?
Advantages of Diversity in the Workplace

I. This design allows each team member to focus on their strengths.

If an employer can create diversity in the workplace, then each worker will have their strengths complement those of everyone else on the team. That means assignments can be handed out with greater specificity so that the quality of the work improves. Supervisors aren't forced to guess at who might be the best option for an assignment because each person has a unique skill that they bring to the table. Diversity in the workplace allows for strengths and weaknesses to be spread out so that their effects are maximized and minimized respectively. No matter what the requirements of a project might be, there is someone who can step up to lead the team toward a successful result.

II. It increases the number of job opportunities for minority workers.

Diversity in the workplace looks at all population demographics when hiring for an open position. That means employers have an opportunity to find the best possible person for a job because they are not limited to a specific group of individuals. This advantage makes it possible to have more women working in society and promotes the hiring of minority groups. It applies at all levels of employment, from the local small business to multinational firms. When everyone has a chance to work if that's what they want to do, then a secondary benefit of this advantage is that it diversifies the wages and productivity of the economy. This process reduces the amount of risk communities face if an unexpected recession were to occur.

III. Employers have more chances to cross-train workers and teams.

Diversity in the workplace creates teams where each person brings a unique strength to work every day. Individuals can specialize in their career, which means their skills and wisdom can be passed along to other team members. Everyone gets to learn and grow each day because there are higher levels of information exposure thanks to the varying backgrounds and educational opportunities each person accomplished. This advantage also has a secondary benefit that involves cultural awareness. When we can understand the complexities of other ethnicities and perspectives, then it becomes easier to find common ground. This process eventually leads to a higher level of innovation and fewer silos and echo chambers.

IV. Companies have access to more talent.

When diversity in the workplace is a top priority for an organization, then supervisors and hiring managers can expand their applicant screening processes to include more people. There are fewer restrictions on geographic location, educational accomplishments, or previous work histories. The top priority in the hiring process focuses on the talent and skills of the individual, and then how that person could fit into the team. Instead of trying to hire the best possible candidate from a group of applicants, diversity in the workplace encourages managers to find the best person for the job.

V. This perspective can help companies to start growing bigger and faster.

Almost 70% of hiring managers in the United States say that the implementation of a diversity initiative was a contributing factor to the growth of their organization. This advantage helps the organization to create new opportunities for existing team members, install new positions, and raise wages as productivity and creativity levels rise to encourage a stronger sales atmosphere. Hiring managers need the tools that can help them to find the best candidates for each person to take advantage of this opportunity. About 90% of supervisors think that the use of cross-border communication allows their company to grow bigger and faster. Nearly half focus on recruiting as a way to improve diversity.

VI. Diversity in the workplace creates more revenue-earning opportunities.

The companies which focus on diversification are the businesses which tend to see more sales and revenues because of their efforts. Emphasizing multiple language fluency for a team can boost their profits by 10% for every fluent language that is spoken. Gender diversity can help revenues grow by 40% in the first year of this effort. This advantage can open new markets for the organization that can help profits to start climbing as well without a significant increase in the work of the team. Diversity in the workplace goes beyond skin color or gender. These benefits occur when lifestyle differences, spiritual perspectives, and other unique life factors are taken into account during the hiring process. You cannot exclude employees from a job because of their differences, but you can look for people who can fit into a specific role for you.

VII. It is a way to increase the creativity of an entire team.

Almost 80% of employees working in the United States say that they are not using their creativity to its full potential. Diversity is one of the best environments to encourage this approach to a career because it offers numerous perspectives that can enhance the brainstorming sessions. The biggest complainers about a lack of creative energy in the modern workplace are those who limit the diversity of their teams. Having different perspectives can create conflict at times, but the unique interpretation of life that each person brings is invaluable to the employer and their team. The need to create change or embrace differences is what leads to an environment that encourages innovation.

VIII. Diversity in the workplace exposes societal bias.

Bias is what destroys diversity in the workplace before it can establish itself. Hiring managers tend to bring men on more than women, even if the qualifications of each candidate are equal. During a study funded by Harvard and Princeton, managers were given a set of applications and qualifications, but they did not reveal the gender of each identity. During this blind process, women were preferred over their male counterparts when gender was not part of the hiring process. Because of this issue, women could be under-represented in the labor force by over 50%. People with an alternative gender identity (outside of male or female) can see even more struggles in this area. It is a problem for racial minorities around the world as well.

IX. Customers are attracted to diversity in the workplace.

Over 40% of employees say that their company has the right amount of diversity or that their teams should try to become more unique. Although it can be challenging to share a workplace environment with someone who is uniquely different, the advantages typically outweigh the problems which can develop over time. When everyone comes from the same perspective, then the daily routine becomes dull. Going to work becomes a boring experience. People can even lose their passion for what they do because there is a lack of diversity present on their team. There are immediate benefits to consider when hiring managers make diversity a top priority. It can lower the levels of burnout which are present in the workplace, improve the quality of each project, and boost the levels of community exposure that are present.

X. Productivity levels improve because of diversity in the workplace.

Even when a team doesn't like the idea of being diverse, their productivity levels can rise by more than 30%. When people have co-workers who are different from them, then there is an increase in the sensitivity levels that are present in the workplace. People start to look for ways to find common ground. There is more time given to each team member to share ideas, and a higher emphasis on hiring women occurs. The fastest way for an employer to encourage a higher level of productivity is to add diversity throughout their organization. Even when there are moments where the work levels decline, the overall benefit never disappears.

List of the Disadvantages of Diversity in the Workplace

I. Hiring managers focus on leadership qualities too often.

Diversity in the workplace seeks out experts who excel in their chosen career, job function, and team environment. The goal is to create a series of strengths that allows everyone to grow over time. These are all advantages, but it can become a problem if hiring managers are bringing in people who all want to be in charge. Competition can be healthy, but it can also be dangerous when it spirals out of control. When the goal is to promote the individual instead of the team, then a diversity initiative fails. You must go beyond what you see to create a team that complements one another. That means there must be leaders, people who are content with their current position, and individuals who come to work because of their passion. There must be emotional diversity too.

II. Diversity can create workers who are over-qualified for some jobs.

Communities grow and decline naturally as the economy settles into a comfortable pattern. Diversity in the workplace can create stable circumstances and more job security, but it can also create a series of problems where workers become over-qualified for what they are doing. If that individual were to lose their job for some reason, then it could become a struggle for them to find new employment elsewhere. We saw this problem throughout the United States during the Great Recession years. Employers were hiring people who were willing to work for almost any wage. You had people who had earned a Ph.D. trying to fill cashier positions at fast-food establishments because there were no job opportunities in their area.

III. Diversity in the workplace can create too many opinions.

When hiring managers focus on diversity, then they are creating a series of differing opinions that can make it easier to find the right journey to take for forward progress. There are also times when the sheer number of available opinions can create a problem for the organization. When everyone gets a chance to be heard, then the speed of a project can slow down just as quickly as it can increase.

IV. Offshoring can become a point of emphasis with diversity in the workplace.

Domestic diversity can become an expensive proposition. It costs a lot, between salary and benefits, to hire the best people for your open positions. Because of this issue, it is not unusual for companies to look for offshoring opportunities that can help them to add unique perspectives to their corporate identity without a significant labor expense. This issue can create a lack of job security for existing workers, which can limit their focus and productivity. Platforms like Upwork and Fiverr bring freelancers into this mix as well. If a company can hire independent contractors at a lower rate to receive equal or superior work, then they will do so. The reason why the middle class is growing around the world is because of diversity initiatives, which means fewer local jobs might be available.

V. Diversity in the workplace can lessen the amount of trust that exists.

When an organization decides to make a diversity initiative a top priority, then there is an immediate decrease in the amount of trust that is present in the workplace. This disadvantage impacts every population demographic – including people who come from the same culture, educational background, and career experience. Although this disadvantage doesn't create silos or team isolation, it can create roadblocks to collaboration. Some people will interact less often with others, experience fear if they are forced to do so, and this issue eventually can limit productivity.

Different perspectives create unique opinions and approaches to life that can create severe disagreements in the workplace. It is not unusual for every person to believe that their individual perspectives are the correct one, so they will share that information with others. If someone should happen to disagree, then some people will take that as a personal attack against their character more easily.

VI. Diversity in the workplace can create communication problems.

People from different cultures may not speak the same language as their primary communication option. Hiring people from different areas can provide unique perspectives, but it can also cause issues with how co-workers speak with one another. Even when the same language is spoken, there can be differences in the meaning of certain words or jargon understanding problems that can create confusion in the workplace.

VIII. Diversity initiatives are usually left to a single person to implement.

About 2 out of every 5 companies leave their diversity initiatives in the hands of a single individual or sponsor. That person is usually the Chief Executive Officer or another member of the leadership team. This assignment is fine if the CEO or another member of the C-suite doesn't have a lot on their plate, but this process is usually put on the back burner of priorities. It is easier to talk about making this issue a priority than to create new policies and procedures that can make it a reality. For the remaining companies that use multiple people to create diversity in the workplace, there can be silos created that individualize this process so that a similar result occurs. There must be complete leadership buy-in for this process to be effective.

IX. Complaint levels often rise with a diversity initiative.

There tends to be more conflict between individual team members in a diverse environment when compared to one where most people come from the same perspective. Different habits and working styles can create bothersome results. Imagine sitting next to a co-worker who needs to click a pen constantly to think, and that's how some people see this process. Without proactive management, an increase in complaints and grievances typically occurs, which means there is more time and money spent on investigations. This disadvantage can become so severe that some companies will see a surge in resignations because they don't like being placed into an "uncomfortable" situation. That means an organization must cope with the necessary costs to replace the lost workers, so it may take months (or years) to recoup the investments made.

On conclusion, diversity in the workplace requires a commitment from every level of the chain of command for it to be a successful experience. If the CEO doesn't buy into the process, then neither will the entry-level worker. Then there must be a monetary commitment given to the process to ensure its successful completion. We live in a society that expects instant results. Diversity can provide unique perspectives, but it may take time for revenue and productivity increases to arrive. Many initiatives stop before they can be successful because there is a lack of patience with this process. The advantages and disadvantages of diversity in the workplace must be carefully managed for the results to be successful.

Q4 What Information Technology Outsourcing brings organizational advantages ?

Information technology outsourcing advantages

In any organization information technology department, information system operations remain the predominant function outsourced, other functions are also being performed by external service providers and the relationship is between outsourcing and certain demographics: size, industry is formation intensity. The results suggest that system operations remain being performed by external service providers. Further, industry and information intensity has some influence on the extent of outsourcing of certain functions.

Information technology department outsoucring benefits may include as below:

The first reason is cost reduction, trying to remain competitive and up-to-date is becoming a financial burden to many organizations. This is true particularly in fields, such as banking and financial services, health care and manufacturing. Hiring outsiders to handle part or even all of its information system often helps an organization to provide better services and maintain a competitive advantage. The information technology industry choice of outsourcing factor is related to size, industry type and information technology.

The second reason is technological and/or human resources in the management of the information technology infrastructure skill improvement. The information technology department outsourcing service to external service provider, includes the degree of internalization of technological resources and the degree of internalization of human resources. Some economists defined internalization of outsourcing service is as ownership is by the focal organization which takes on full control with profit and loss responsibility. Also who define outsourcing is as involving a significant use of resources, either technological and/or human resources, external to the organizational hierarchy in the management of the information technology infrastructure.

So the information technology external service providers includes: applications development and maintenance, systems operations, networks/telecommunications management and user computing support, system planning and management purchase of application software, but excludes business consulting services, after-sale vendor services and the lease of telephone lines etc. outsourcing services.

The third reason is economics of scale in areas of hardware, software. This pressure is seen as the most significant factor driving today's corporate interest. An outsourcing service provision might be in a position to exploit economics of scale in areas of hardware, software and staff since it pools different kind of technological projects from many service receivers. Outsourcing information technological service can reduce the corporate's cost with the high level of IT investment, there are increasing pressures to move away from fixed expenditure, corporate overhead towards a more direct variable cost approach to control the IT operations.

The IT costs can become predictable for overruns is often placed on the service provider. Outsourcing service can allow the service to gain immediate access to competitiveness in delivering products or services as well as to avoid of obsolescence risk, due to the changes in the nature of the IT infrastructure, the risk of obsolescence is high. Outsourcing can allow the service provider has the ability to diversify these risks across a broad range of service receivers. However, long term contracts might in spread the risk, the weakness is back to the receiver.

It seems outsourcing IT service has also these disadvantages: such as, loss of flexibility or managerial control. Outsourcing reduces real or perceived control over both quality real or perceived control over both the quality of software and the timetable of project since the work is now being carried out by people not under direct supervision.

It also threats to long term career prospects to information system professionals because many of them do not find suitable. Is jobs or promising career paths in both areas of the corporation. Outsourcing also increases coordination cost.

It may requires increasing time to communicate and coordinate with the service provider. Traditionally, the formal meeting cost of negotiating and monitoring the outsourcing contract are potentially wide ranging, indirect and substantial increasing, such as, additional releasing or transferring employees, in license transfer by software vendors and in re-negotiating contracts costs. So, the IT industry of profit motivates service provider might not be in the least interests of the outsourcing service receivers. Some IT service providers are in the business of maximizing their profit at any cost, this could run counter to a service receiver's interest.

Q5 How can Outsourcing or insourcing in human resource bring organizational advantages?

To choosing of outsourcing or insourcing in human resource supply chain factor of the controlling service demanders needs to concern this issues: Should human resource activities be provided in house or should all or past of those activities be outsourced? The relationship between organizational structure and the HR function is an important variable. The individual activities that comprise HR systems include not only the employee life cycle from recruiting to termination, but also planning for organizational staffing needs and improving organizational effectiveness.

How organizations need to outsource HR function to not care employees knowledge and skill is a factor to influence any organizations choose to outsourcing non core employees when which have no any right employees to be promoted to do the position. For example, firms engage in HR outsourcing to reduce management access HR expertise, achieve workforce flexibility, focus managerial resources and keep up with changing workplace negotiations. Also, supporting the tend is the availability of common technology platform, which can reduce costs for organizations and risks. However, organizations are afraid of losing some control over delivery of outsourcing services and finding themselves dependent on the vendor or liable for the vendors actions where there are both benefits and challenges may be informed by the structure of the relationship between client firms and these organizations offering the outsourced activities to client firms.

What variables are impacted by HR outsourcing of staffing? Which include: administrative costs for labor expense, client firm to HR relations, HR regulatory competency requirement, knowledge of cost factors, e.g. billing and pay rates, vendor markups and margins, vendor management competency requirement, client and vendor relationship, communication is between client managers and staffing vendor, employee data-available, data quality control, data security, match with job requirement, employee quality, inter-vendor competition, mining of client talent by vendor , quality content for preferred staffing vendor, standardization of business process (intra-company), strategic focus of client firm, demands on client managers vendor competency and external economic environmental viability.

However, it has dynamic relationship between the client firms and staffing vendors. Moreover, the models of human resource supply chain, every has different set of advantages and disadvantages for the client firms. The models can be relate to the decision making process on outsourcing of human resources. As strategic services tactic decisions have an important impact or selecting the particular HR outsourcing model that a client firm adopter.

The another model is the balance of power and control over managing the control workers differ to decide what every worker individual skills or abilities outsourcing demand. Moreover, local contracting is also the predominant traditional model for outsourcing staffing with non-core employees. A client firm usually uses several staffing vendors to meet temporary staffing needs for seasonal functions, employee absences and special projects. The advantages of local contracting are high touch and high quality of service by staffing vendors, minimal bureaucracy, empowerment of hiring any high qualified employees to get the job done, and a relatively better fit between specific staffing vendors and functional needs.

Q6 What are the disadvantages of local contracting to organizations?
The disadvantages of local contracting

The disadvantages of local contracting can increase costs from non-standardization of hiring practices and procedures across the client form, a significant amount of word of mouth and subjective quality issues, high local costs and client firm us subjected to the capabilities of the staffing vendors and contract employees. However, local HR contracting is the most flexible, high quality, but expense, inefficient and ineffective HR outsourcing model for the client firm. Another model is the working period to be decided to outsource HR contracting. In this situation, in the short term and on a day-to-day basis, the client firm aims to achieve on economy of scale with its staffing vendors. The total costs of temporary workers as well as internal costs for contracting with several different vendors are higher than if it needs one staffing vendors to meet all its needs. So, the client company can set the reasonable pricing that it pays for its temporary outsourcing staffs. Each staffing vendor secures a different rate range with each vendor as opposed as one contact. In the long term, it is benefiting, each specialized staffing vendor is able to fully work with each function needs temporary utilization is better than the average. Mismatches are fewer. Functional departments are able to receive a high quality / high touch service in any time period. Another model is the centralizing is when the department standardizes the staffing process to drive costs down of temporary workers. This tends to occur when a percentage of non-core employees reach a certain ratio of core employees. The advantages include more uniform standards in hiring process, billing rates and pay rates, departmental hiring managers can refocus their effort to choose outsourcing staffing, criteria may be established for a performed suppliers list and greater security for the staffing established vendors that offer higher quality services. The disadvantages include new departmental responsibilities in HR which decreases outsourcing efficiencies for the organizations daily administrative direction is rather than long term strategic direction. Usually lacking qualifications to fulfill the responsibilities, overall, centralizing of HR outsourcing is that firms can achieve more standardization which additional bureaucratic costs and the necessary non-core jobs do not get done as a need. Another model is purchasing HR, which manages staffing vendors from HR to the purchasing unit of an organizations. The goal is to continue cost reductions by increasing efficiencies. In conclusion, the main benefits of HR outsourcing include maintaining organizational control over the hiring process, application of purchasing capabilities for greater standardization in hiring processes pay rates and bill rates. So, any outsoucred HR organizations may be reduce hiring process cost.

Q7 How can global outsourcing source strategy to bring a value supply chain advantages to organizations?

What is global outsourcing source strategy in a departmental role? In a highly competitive global environment, many manufacturers are responded by setting and outsourcing relations for components and finished products with lower cost producers on a contractual electronic commerce department, (original equipment manufacturer basis). Outsourcing strategy is part of the value supply chain of corporate activated. Nowadays, global outsourcing increases organizational and technological capacity of firms and cooperating a network of remotely located external suppliers performing.

These understanding the important roles that product designers, engineers and production managers and purchasing manager etc. play in global sourcing strategy empowerment. Specially, electronic commerce is popular to supply chain. For example, Toyota car manufacturing company, owns unique capabilities by designing and manufacturing certain car components in-house , i.e. insourcing. Toyota also outsource manufacturing activities, Toyota adopts purchasing necessary, but no strategic inputs from independent component suppliers on obtaining a lower cost for these inputs. For example, products would be belts, tires and batteries to vehicle products that are not customized and do not differentiate its products from its competitors. Toyota's outsourcing strategy is car strategic inputs provide differentiation, e.g. engine, transmission etc. are sources from suppliers based on strategic partnership to gain to access to suppliers' capabilities and it is also a conceptualize global outsourcing sourcing strategy to Toyota car manufacturing company.

How value chain outsourcing affects firm level performance. Global outsourcing strategy means to identify which production units that will serve which particular markets and how components will be supplied for production and thus included a number of basic choices, companies can make in decision how to serve various markets. Either choice relates to the use of inputs, assembly or production within the country to serve a foreign market or decides to use of internal or external supplies of components or finished products. In this outsourcing source input situation, the term sourcing is needed to describe how multi-national companies mange in of components and finished products in serving foreign and domestic markets. Sourcing decision making is both contractual point of view, the sourcing of major components and products are occurred by multi-national companies. First is from parents or their foreign subsidiaries. Second is from independent suppliers on a contractual basis. The first type of sourcing is known as insourcing. Otherwise, the second type of sourcing is referred to outsourcing. How to achieve economies of scale by outsourcing or insourcing sourcing input strategy? Therefore, the two outsourcing strategies are multi-faceted and require careful examination.

The two economists (Abrahamson & Rosenkopf, 1993) indicated that In long term, outsourcing can help to reduce fixed investment in finance view point, in-house manufacturing facilities and thus lower the breakeven point, which subsequently helps boost an outsourcing company whose return on equity (ROE). Thus, if any one corporate performance is evaluated on the basis of its contribution to the company's ROE.

Also, in the short term or long term on resource inputs outsourcing view, early adopters of outsourcing strategy indeed experienced efficiency gains as they were able to reduce fixed investment in in-house manufacturing facilities and lows their ROE. But, later adopters may have different to gain institutions legitimacy or because of competition pressures in the industry, despite some inherent uncertainties about the long term costs and benefits of outsourcing strategy. It seems that outsourcing strategy was devised as any organization's policy makers to access trade linkages of benefits for short term or long term.

Outsourcing strategy is a systematic analysis of the economic, political and regulatory implications indicates potential benefits along with a number of potentially negative side effects to any organizations. Then, outsourcing strategy will be caused this question: How to assess the risks and benefits of outsourcing for organizational sectors and nations both? The decision to change outsourcing behavior to carry a business activity may have profound implications for outsourcer and outsource receiver both, but little impact of the sector level. The common occurrence of industry decisions to outsource most manufacturing, including sale of factories, it created a new sub-sector, contract manufacturing. Otherwise, at a national level and public sectors become less distinct to outsourcing strategy. Public policy on outsourcing has stimulated extensive debate, privatization social justice and value for money etc. challenges.

Q8 How to motivate outsourcing, evidence of what is being outsourced risk and concerns to impact organizational behavioral change ?

Outsourcing activities include: outsources manufacturing components and other value adding activities. Some focused on employment is outsourced another firm's employees carrying out tasks previously performed one's own employees. Outsourcing is an activity outside the organization's chosen core competencies. It seems outsourcing is a sub-contracting relationships between firms, all foreign production, hiring of workers in non-traditional jobs, such as control workers and temporary and part time workers.

What are the motivations for outsourcing reasons? Why outsourcing is needed to any organization. For example, it can enable firms to focus on core activities. The concept of focus originates in operation on a small, manageable, number of tasks at which the operation becomes excellent to specific technologies and as a risk of vertical integration advantages. Other benefits of outsourcing appear is literature on strategic management, operations management, purchasing and supply and innovations. Moreover, outsourcing can improve flexibility to meet changing business conditions, demands for products, services and technologies by creating smaller and more flexible clear evidence includes improved creditability image, greater workforce flexibility and avoiding being backed into specific assets and technologies are harder to measure. How outsourcing can improve company performance. For airline manufacturing industry example, Hill & Jones (1995) showed that the manufacture of a large portion of the Boeing 767 is Boeing's third largest commercial aircraft, which is outsourced to Japanese manufacturers, which include Fuji, Kawasaki and Mitsubish. As a result, only 10% of the value of the 767 Boeing is produced in-house. So, outsourcing is an attempt to enhance manufacturing air place industry competitiveness.

How can choose smarter outsourcing? Organizations hope to do sight options to save money, among themselves staff layoffs and a reduction of overhead costs, such as office space. Private companies have long outsourced in order to save time and money. During periods of economic growth, many organizations began to use outsourcing more frequently and staff workloads grew in proportion to increase budgets. Tasks such as conducting needs assessments, reviewing proposals, conducting site visits, monitoring and creating evaluations systems were increasingly given to outside contractors, consulting firms and independent consultants in the belief that external specialists could do the work more efficiently and effectively than company itself.

Nowadays, there is a growing stream of organizations need to research into the outsourcing of innovation activities within the innovation, management, marketing and economics disciplines. These organizations need to understand how with the outsourcing practice becoming more commonplace in their industry. However, their behaviors bring these two questions: Whether outsource or internalize innovation activities and the performance implications of this decision can support for both transaction cost and resource based arguments is examined with both theory bases showing substantial attention?

Whether outsourcing innovation activities can lead to faster product development and cost savings? On advantages hand, it is possible that outsourcing may lead to higher costs and slower new product development. Further the technological uncertainty may have conflicting impacts on the outsourcing decision that are not yet well understand. When outsourcing product development has reduced costs and has proved speed to market. On disadvantages hand, outsourcing has also reduce product development time delays and higher quality concerns. Why to cause performance implications of outsourced innovation activities in transaction in cost economics and the resource-based view point? When outsourcing product development has been to reduce costs and has improved speed to market, outsourcing product development is not unlike other make or buy decisions. So, make vs buy decision is similar to logistic and IT outsourcing. Internalization of product development will be preferred when transaction costs are excessive. Otherwise, the market i.e. outsourcing will be selected when transaction costs are low. Transaction costs can include adaption, safeguarding and measurement costs. Adaption costs represent efforts to adjust contract to change conditions and are a result of environmental uncertainty.

When a firm may have to revise on agreement with a partner company, this facing substantial penalties, due to an unstable market environments, the firm is likely to perform this function internally. Safeguarding costs characterize the costs of an outsourcing provider acting opportunities after investments have been made in the inter-firm relationship and are the result of transaction specific investment. Measurement costs include all expenses with confirming that contracts have been fulfilled passably. The contracting firm may face substantial costs to estimate quality for contractual services. When the sum total of these transaction costs is substantial, internalization will be favored.

Q9 How does environmental uncertainty factor influence organizational behavioral change ?

Environmental uncertainty refers to unanticipated changes in circumstances surrounding an exchange in market uncertain and technological uncertainty. Market uncertainty is the fluctuation and unpredictability of demand. With respect to innovation projects, market uncertainty may cause frequent changes to the development, complications and adding expense to external contracting. These changes may necessitate renegotiation or cancellation of innovation contracts, which will likely carry prohibitive penalties (a term) transaction costs. These transaction costs promote internalization under high levels of market uncertainty. Otherwise, technological uncertainty environments, selecting market governance allows firms the flexibility to end relationship should technical requirements shift. It seems that market and technological external change factor will influence to benefits to any organizations to choose outsourcing strategy. On the other side, outsourcing can bring this question: Whether the offshore outsourcing of information technology jobs choice is suitable to any IT organizations? Nowadays. The offshore outsourcing if IT jobs from the United States has been enabled by a powerful influence of global economic demographic and technological forces. In fact, many IT companies were drawn to offshoring outsourcing because of the need for programmers to fix the Y2K problem in the late 1990- year. It is shortages of US programmers.

Other factors driving this phenomenon include the wage gap between the US and developing countries, e.g. China and India, advances in technology, labor availability, expanding foreign markets and foreign government incentives. The spread of the offshoring phenomenon from low skill manufacturing to high wage white collar service industry jobs reduces the country's IT jobs critics, it represents the mobility for many US workers who saw post-secondary education as the route to a higher standard of living. The offshoring outsourcing of manufacturing and service jobs from the US to lower cost foreign nations become a national issue in a very short time. The impact of offshore outsource on the information technology sector gives outsourcing potential loss of millions of jobs at all wage levels and the critical contribution is the IT sector to US productivity growth. However, decisions about the locations of manufacturing or service facilities reflect market forces key factors include the size of local markets, capital availability and costs, labor availability skill levels and cost, logistic issues, reliability and infrastructure and IT in particular relationships with research institutions. All these factors will influence the choice of offshore outsource IT jobs strategy top any organizations.

Q10 Can outsourcing bring what benefit of work skills to organizations ?

Whether outsourcing will bring what kind of work skills. Many employers choose outsourcing to employ employees. This core of our work is identifying trends which will transform global society and the global marketplace. How it influences our nature of work form health care to technology, the work place and human identity. A decade ago, workers worried about jobs being outsourced overseas. Today companies, such as Odesk and Liveops can assemble teams " in the cloud" to dosales, customer support and many other tasks. It seems outsoucring can influence many high technological job of changes. Global connectivity, smart machines and new media are just some of the drivers reshaping how we thank about work, what constitutes work and the skills, we shall need to be productive contributors in the future. As computer technology in the cloud will be used popularly to society. A signal is typically a small or local innovation that has the potenial to grow in scale and geographic distribution. A signal can be a new product, a new practice, a new market strategy, a new policy or new technology, such as online cloud computing files storage service method. It is an innovative social science method to computer users. However, this new computer files storage method influences outsourcing service of needs increasing. It will have key drivers and skills areas that will be most relevant to the technological workforce of the future.

It is estimates that by 2025 year, the number of Americans over 60 age will increase by 70%. The challenge of an aging population will come. What it means to age, individuals will need to rearrange their approach to their career, family life and education to accommodate their life plan. Increasing, people will work long past 65 age in order to have adequate resources for retirement. Multiple careers will be commmplace and lifelong learning to prepare for occupational change will see major growth. To take advantage of this well experienced organizations will have to rethink the traditional career paths in organizations, creating more diversity and flexibility. As the high technological cloud computing storage method is invented. Any organizations can save their files to the central cloud computer storage system website to save or find their files from website more easily. It will reduce their computer department expenditure and staff salary. So, outsourcing computer file storage service demands will be influenced to increase to any organizations as well as organizations will reorganize their computer department job nature to shape the kinds of social, economic and political organizations which inhabit. Outsourcing is a good solve method to assist organizations to pay cheap salary to employ many retired high age workers by contract or temporary or part time method to reduce their computer department's number of employees and the retired labors only need to pay cheap salary to learn how to use internet to help whose employers to save their files to their outsourcing computer storage service provider's central computer storage system every day efficiently.

So, organizations do not need to employ many computer department staffs to avoid to pay much salaries to this computer department expenditure. They can choose outsourcing to pay cheap salaries to employ many retirement labors to assist them to do simple office storage job from internet channel efficiently and effectively. Hence, internet high technological innovation can influence office outsoucing of job duties increasing.

Whether domestic outsoucing in the America, what assesses trends and effects on job quality. Nowadays, US firms' use of contractors and independent contractors and its effect on job quality and inequality. Why firms choose contract out for certain functions and assess their predictions about likely impacts on job quality, stagnant wages, growing inquality and the deterioration of job quality are among the most important challenges facing the US economy today. Although any country's domestic outsourcing , firms' use of contractors, franchises and independent contractors any one of these factors is a potentially important influence to companies reduce compensation and shift economy risk to workers. However, the domestic outsoucing takes place on a much larger scale and effects many more workers than has been recognized ranging from low wage service workers, security guards, warehouse workers and hotel housekeepers to professionals and technical workers, such as programmers, health care technicians and accountants. These tends are part of structural change in the organization of production to influence quality of jobs and the nature of employment contract after outsourcing jobs are popular. The quality of jobs include wages, benefits, employee skills and training and mobility opportunities and job security as well as inequality across jobs. Domestic outsoucing concerns these issues: such as employment and labor law, the provision of health, pension and other workplace benefits. However, any companies choose outsourcing of employment reasons include, such as that it relates how management choices to pursue value added or cost focused strategies. Contracting out is difficult to define because a large part ot economic activity has always occurred through business-to-business transactions, as captured in macro-economic input-output models. Outsoucing job employment method can influence any one labor's individual quality of jobs. Usually, international companies choose the offshoring of work in global supply chains. Until recently, the domestic counterpart outsourcing employment method has grown supply chains to domestic or regional outsoucing employment.

What factors cause domestic outsourcing and whether firm decisions about what to retain in-house and what to outsource have changes over time. Some evidence suggests that firms have responded by focusing on their core competencies and outsourcing low value added tasks as well as higher value added specialized functions. Advanced technologies have facilitated this process by allowing firms to outsource entire functions ans more easily monitor contractors as well as employees who work, leading to new forms of networked production and rise of specialized outsouring employment firms. Domestic outsoucing influences the changes of job quality, benefits, hours, workload, job stability, schedule stability and occupational safety, health, incidence of wage theft and access to training and promotions. Predictions are less clear for job requiring professional or technicial or specialized skills or those that are outsourced to large and diversified outsourced contractors. Types of outsourced contracts include: suppliers or vendors of products, such as manufacturing inputs or services, such as business services or staffs service or staffing firms, franchisees and independent contract, such as freelancers, independent contracts or non demand platform outsourced workers. It is significant restructuring of domestic manufacturing supply chains will greater reliance on suppliers and subcontractors. In addition, the potential growth of on demand outsourcing work as well as other forms of job fragmentation. It causes this question: How outsourced workers are multiple forms of income generating work to achieve economic security and how outsourcing workers can build career across jobs and over time.

Firm in every sector of the economy contract with other firms as part of their production process, as do governmental entities. The functions that are outsourced vary widely. For example: human resources ans research and development functions, building services, recycling, regulation and compliance, accounting, credit card collection, call centres, mortage and check processing, information technology and data processing, logistics and transportation, machine maintenance, cable installation, food services, food processing, parts manufacturing and assembly, laundry and housekeeping etc. outsourced jobs causes.

Whether what business impact of outsourcing will be caused? Nowadays, IT outsourcing was clearly a part of an effective management strategy that the companies felt IT outsourcing strategy can bring to achieve positive results. Information technology outsourcing providing servicers will be predicted to provide services that is expected to raise over the next five years minimum. The companies demand clients expected benefits of IT outsourcing and determined that cost reduction, increased operation, efficiency and improved IT effectiveness. What are the impacts of outsourcing to influence better long-term improvement in the business performance? It is impossible to being benefits of significant reduction and lower growth in sellings, general and administrative expense to IT outsourcing company demand clients. Also, pre-existing corporate cultures are focused on business improvement to IT outsourcing company demand clietns. In the past researches, some economists indicated that points can be used to reflect the actual numbers increase or decrease in percent. However, their prior researches shows that prior to outsourcing, the annual growth in selling, general and administration expenses of eompanies in the study was already 4.2 points lower than sector medium. Moreover, within one to two years after IT outsourcing these companies improved even most.

Annual growth in selling and general administrative expenses for them was 9.9 points lower efford to assist any IT outsourcing will have selling and administrative expenses for long term. Also, almost two-third of the companies studied outperformed in increased growth in return on asset two to three years after IT outsourcing commenced. Prior to outsourcing, the annual ROA growth rate for companies in the study ws 7.5 points lower than the sector median. After outsourcing, however these companies experienced 8.6 points higher median a substantial change of 16.1 points. Also, nearly two to third of the companies studied grew earnings faster than their peers. Two to three years after IT outsourcing, companies experienced an annual rate of growth in earnings 11.8 points higher than the growth rate of the sector median. Thus, it seems IT outsourcing can assist the IT outsourcing demand clients to reduce expenditure and to raise income both as the same time. Then, it will cause these questions to IT outsourcing demand clients. Is outsourcing influencing in an economic downturn to finance sector in the short term? Is the finance sector's renewed change for outsourcing just a temporary cost-cutting measure? Will today's economic climate initiate long term financial and productivity gains?

Whether what are benefits and disadvantages of outsourcing finance sector IT. I shall demonstrate why outsourcing open source software support and maintenance can be a good choice to start. Firstly when company plans to budget cuts expenditures, IT outsourcing is often the first choice. For example in 2003 year, Zurich Financial services' sprawling IT department consisted of more than 7,500 employees. After posting a record loss of 3.4 billion the year before, Zurich decided to cut down on in those staff and outsource nearly half of its IT work. Outsourcing has successfully cut costs by 45 percent and cut the number of in house IT staff by 60 percent. Here are some of the benefits that companies enjoy when they outsource information technology functions to competent, reliable vendors.

In fact, it can be too expensive to maintain, company's own information technology, especially during a recession. Fortunately, many IT functions can be easily and efficiently outsourced, positively impacting individual company's bottom line. Employee costs are much higher than just salary and benefits, keeping employees happy, productive and busy takes time, effort and money. Although, many IT staffs will be dismissed, it will increase the unemployment ratio in societies. But, moving an IT service out of house means financial organizations don't have to worry about technology refresh costs in the future. It also cuts down on human resources requirements, specialist IT service provides which can provide the newest technologies and deliver quality service more than company itself in house information provides are the most effective to develop and implement and upgrade their clients' software or the launch on a new platform, due to the expert's time is wasted on day-to-day duties for whose other IT outsourcing demand clients. However, instead of IT outsourcing service outsourced offshoring in that service sector, how economic impact to influence the outsourced offshoring country. For example, United States continues to run an international trade surplus in services. Many Americans are particularly concerned about the loss of skilled, well paid jobs in such fields as computer programming and accounting etc. positions. These jobs seemed relatively secure at a time when many manufacturing jobs were being cost to import competition. Similarly, telephone call centers, once viewed as an esonomic development opportunity in some areas, increasingly are moving low wage countries, such as India and the Philippines. Thus, offshoring raises many questions for policymakers and general public. For example, which service jobs will be affected most by import competition. What are the likely effects of service-sector offshoring on U.S.A. output, employment and our standard of living, such as America? Is offshoring really a problem that requires restrictive government actions or are other kinds of policies more appropriate to give Americans or other countries the highest possible living standard?

The term of offshoring refers to the relocation of jobs and production to a foreign country. The relocated jobs and production could be at a foreign office of the same multinational company or at a separate company located abroad. In constrast, the term outsourcing doesn't necessary imply that jobs and production are relocated to another country. The major outsourcing service jobs include human resource, accounting and information technology etc. in-house service jobs in large organizations. However, the loss of service jobs and factory production is caused by offshoring is diffuclt to measure. It is also difficult to determine the impact of offshoring on total services employment in the United States or other countries. International trade in services covers a wide range of industries and activites. For example, travel and transportation includes travel expenditures, passenger fares and frieght and port services, royalties and license fees cover transactions including patents, copyrights, trademarks and other intangible proprietary rights to use, produce or distribute products.

Other private services include many of these industries, such as education, financial services insurance, telecommunications and other professional services etc. Some economists indicated that occupational employment statistics for the Unisted States provided additional evidence that past service sector offshoring had been small. About 14 million service jobs were at risk of offshoring in 2000 year, when about 96 million service jobs had a low risk of ofshoring. The decline in the at-risk service occupations from 2000 year to 2002 year was about 218,000 jobs or roughly 109,000 jobs annually, relatively small number that is consistent with the estimates of McCarthy or Zandi.

In percentage terms, employment in the at risk occupations fell at a faster rate from 2000 year to 2002 year than in the low risk occupations. This faster decline is consistent with offshoring activity, although the decline is consistent with other explanations as well, such as faster of technological change in industries employing the risk occupations or greater cyclical sensitivity in these industries. Because offshoring was not the only cause of job loss in the risk occupations, the number of jobs moved offshore was undoubtedly less than 109,000 jobs annually. However, the estimates may understate the total impact because domestic companies with expanding worldwide employment may have located may of their newly created jobs abroad even when they didn't reduce their US employment. Some of those foreign jobs might provide services to US customers and potentially foreign jobs might provide service to US . Conversely, the estimates may overstate the total job loss from offshoring of the foreign outsourcing of some support jobs prevents the loss of other domestic jobs by keeping US firms competitive in world markets. For example, cost reductions from offshoring IT jobs might help a US financial services company win foreign contracts, preserving many professionals and support jobs in the US.

Lower production costs in foreign countries are a major cause of service sector offering. Although, the costs of land and other resources may be cheaper abroad, but the main difference betweeb the US and developing countries is labor costs. There is a large gap in computer programmer wages between the US and other countries. Any organizational capital includes both physical capital, such as machinery and computers and human capital , such as skills and knowledge. The cost savings is come from offshoring also might be reduced if the firm needed to pay higher transportation and telecommunication costs or management spends more time on service quality and data security. Still, the much lower levels of wages ans benefits in developing countries suggests that many services can be produced abroad at lower cost. The in-house professional relocation of labor-intensive service activities, such as legal transcription services to countries with lower labor costs is consistent with economists' basic theory of international trade, comparative advantage. So, in-house outsourced professional service will be a corporative advantage, if the country's legal profession is poor level to compare with the another country. e.g. the skill in-house the legal professional labors of the developing country, such as China is poor educational level to compare with the developed country, such as US. So, if China large organizations chose to outsource themselves in-house legal service jobs to outsource offshoring to US legal professional lawyers to do. It can bring comparative advantage to China large outsourced in-house legal service organizations, due to these China outsourced large organizations can reduce to employ to pay too much salaries to these many in-house Chinese domestic lawyers and the US outsourced legal consultants whose can give more professional legal recommendation to serve to the China large organizations.

In conclusion, although offshoring strategy can increase unemployment chance for this disadvantge. But, all of outsourcing benefits weighs are more than the offsourcing disadvantages. However, outsourcing strategy can have these benefits to the outsourced service demanders. Such as outsourcing is no longer just about cost saving, it is also a strategic tool that may power the twenty first century global economy. Moreover, outsourcing can increase productivity and competitiveness, e.g. for every 1000 jobs British Airways sends to India , the airline saves $23 million, companies can devote a portion of their outsourcing savings to helping employees make job transitions, also leader can no longer afford to view outsourcing as a business tactic, it is now essential to remain competitive. On the world stage, workers now compete globally, so individuals must continually learn more to vie successfully with their peers worldwide, the average company only spends about 20% of the value of its outsourcing contracts to manage its relationship with the outsource provider. So, in the positive view point, outsourcing strategy can bring a potential primary driver of the global economy development. Although, outsourcing can also cause the raising of domestic unemployment chance. But companies may soon be more outsourced than in sourced, signifying a fundamental reorganization that will affect employees, managers, customers and executives. Customers' choice will increase product costs will drop and workers' roles will change. Finally, the most important, the developing country will earn comparative advantage from the developed country's employers' offshoring jobs provision. Thus, the developing country's unemployment rate will be reduced, then the global economy will be kept more balance fairly.

Q11 How future organizational skill needs how to change to bring positive workforce
advantages to employees ?

In the future whether in general organizations need what kinds of employees' skills, they expect employee individual own. It is one interesting question. The common skills that employees need to own in order to any duties to any organizational departments efficiently, e.g. human resource, marketing, administrative, logistic etc. different departments. For hospital, school, business, professional occupations etc. different organizations. Whether future school ought implement one system educational method to teach different common skills to students in order to let them to leave schools to jobs more easier.

Future employers need to create new technologies including automation and algorithms, in order to create new high quality jobs and improve the job quality and productivity of the existing work of human employees in any organizations, e.g. accounting department will need intelligence (AI) to assist account clerks to do simple repeating accounting job tasks in order to share their work load and raise performance efficiency or legal organizations will need (AI) to assist law clerks to do simple repeating legal draft or legal document revising job tasks . All future general clerical jobs will apply (AI) technological tools to assist human to job, it will produce a comprehensive platform for managing workforce change.

Hence, human manual(employees) need to learn how to adopt (AI) job participation to assist them to do different kinds of simple clerical jobs in any organizational administrative departments . They , clerical employees or white color workers need to learn how manage or dominate (AI) tool to improve job performance to be better. However, (AI) administrative workforce change, it is not only one kind of job automation change role in any physical offices. It influences future administrative clerks need change a more flexible manner, utilizing remote staffing beyond physical offices and decentralization of operations organizational workforce change.

Instead of (AI) participation to administrative job aspect, (AI) will also participate to manufacturing industry environment aspect, a new human-machine manufacturing workforce change will exist to any factories, warehouses working environment. Scientists predict that in present an average of 71% of total task hours across the industries are performed by humans, compared a 29% by machines. In this average is expected to have shifted to 58% task hours performed by humans and 42% by machines. In fact, nowadays, in terms of total working hours, no work task was yet estimated to be predominantly performed by a machine or an algorithm (AI). But, this picture is predicted to have somewhat changed with machines and algorithms (AI) on average increasing their contribution to specific tasks by

57% . For example, in the future, 62% of organization's information and data processing and information search and transmission tasks will be performed by machines compared to 46% today.

Therefore, these high technological skillful job change will bring negative influence to some demotive-skillful or low skillful labors to be dismissed, if they can not upgrade or raise or reskillgul their skill level to improve their analytical thinking , technology design and programming skills to cooperate with (AI) tools to work efficiently together in any organizational manufacturing or offie work environment. Because it will have many employers apply (AI) automation tools to participate with blue -color or whiate -color workers' tasks in order to raise efficiencies or improve performance in any working environment. So, it is right time to young or mid age employees need to upskill and/or reskill their rihgt type of skills to prepare future technology risch work environment changeing needs.

Future technological advances will permit an increasing number of tasks traditionally performed by humans to become automated. It seems that , such automation focused primarily on routine tasks, e.g. clerical work, bookkeeping, basic paralegal work and reporting etc. However, with the advent of big data, artificial intelligence (AI), the internet of things and ever-increasing computing power , i.e. the digital revolutions, non-routine tasks are also increasingly likely to become automated. For example, the recent development in robotics and 3D printing allow firms in advanced economies to locate production closer to domestic markets in fully aumomated factories. As a result, the future strongest incentive to automate because of their relatively higher labour costs will be reduced, when production automated will bring the negative influence to dismiss some foolish or low produtive or low skill workers , the owning high automated productive skillful workers will replace the low productive skillful workers in any factories' manufacturing environments. So, technological progress participates to raise quantity of jobs will cause result in significant job losses to low skillful workers. Because future employers will need many high automated productive employees to help them to cooperate with (AI) automated machine to work together efficiently. For example, many proportion of occupations at high risk is greatest in Germany and lowest in Korea, these countries organizations will accept to spend technology investments and education of workers to prepare future automatability manufacturing development successfully.

However, future automatability manufacturing development will bring technological unemployment in possible, due to workers need to adjust to the challenge of automation by switching tasks. Thus, preventing technological unemployment, also technological change does not just destroy jobs, but also generates new roles through its effect on productivity and the demand for new technologies. For example, it has been estimated that, for each high tech-job created in the industries , such as computing equipment or electrical machinery, some 4.9 % additional jobs are created for lawyers, taxi, drivers and waites in the local economy (Moretti, 2011).

Therefore, automated will also influence service industries' job nature change, e.g. taxi drivers need to apply (AI) automated machines to assist them to drive their taxis. When the passenger tells the taxi driver where he/she wants to go. Then, the (AI automated machine will follow the GPS road direction map to be indicated how to drive the taxi to go to the destination automatically . So, future taxi driver is one assistance role to assist the (AI) automated driving tool to dominate the (AI) tool to drive the taxi to catch the passenger to arrive the destination safety in the short time in possible. For another example, future restaurant waiters will need (AI) automated machines's assistance to help them to deliver or dispatch any foods and soft drinks to send to the identified eater's table carefully in accurate and efficient service performance way from the kitchen, in especially in the busy time and many people are sitting in the large size restaurant environment. So, future, waiter roles will be the leader , they need to manage or control or supervise the (AI) robotics how to make decisions to arrange to dispatch which foods or soft drinks to the different tables in preference immediately. Also, future law clerks need to supervise or manage the law robotics how to help them to make decisions to do revision or draft or filing legal tasks in preference in order to avoid any typing words are mistaken to type on computers or revised draft in wrong way to assist manual legal clerks' mistaken words are appearanced on any legal documents. So, the law clerk future role will be the trainer role , he/she eeds to teacher the robots how to check any words, e.g. grammers to correct them to be right grammers, or giving the accurate revision legal documents' instruction to let the legal robots to know how to revise each legal draft to prove whether which part of the legal draft will have wrong to be needed to revise.

In conclusion, future many manual workers' service or manfacturing job natures will become automated assistance to robotics. So, employees need to upgrade their skills in order to adopt new technological work nature change.

Reference

Moretti, E. (2011) local labor market in O, Ashentelter and D. Card (eds.) handbook of labor economics, Elsevier, North Halland.

Q12 What are regional dynamic skills influence global any organizational labour market demand ?

Businessmen expect to improve better economic environment, they will prefer to recruit the most sought after skills of intelligent employees to bring positive beneficial impact to organizations. However, technology and digisation has had a significant influence on workers. Future globalization will trend digital economic development. Hence, it will influence workers' skills to be changed also. In fact, not all changes are positive because some workers will possible lose jobs, either due to new technology replaces their jobs or they lack enough effort to improve their skills in global digital economic labour market environment.

It brings this question: What are regional dynamic skills need whn digital busines environment is growing. In fact, organizations will continue to deal with skills shortages, labour markets across the global are continually changing. so, more employers and workers will need to adopt innovate working pattern, e.g. on call jobs, freelance jobs will grow popularly. The greater flexibility afforded to employ regardly.

Finally, digitalisation includes artificial intelligence, big data , online platforms. All these new technology will influence future employees how to worker. For example, they can apply online platform to work at home conveniently. So, they do not need to go to offices. They can finish their jobs and send to their employers by email easily. This kinds of job pattern can raise efficiencies and employers do not need go to offices often.

An important implication of innovating working which needs the employees who own digital skills in order to serve organizations more efficiently. So, employers are increasingly able to access demographics that were hitherto less active in labour markets. For example, future more women are joining the labour market because part time and self employment opportunities make it easier. This kinds of job pattern can raise efficiencies and employees do not need go to offices often.

An important implication of innovating working which needs the employees who own digital skills in order to serve organizations more efficiently. So, employers are increasingly able to access demographic that were hitherto less active in labour markets. For example, future more women are joining the labour market because part time and self employment opportunities make it easier to manage family with work life. So, digital skilling needs will cause many women lose jobs in possible. If the women lack digital job skills. Because high digital skill occupations need, like those requiring research, medical treatment and architectural design occupational digital skills are more common in the services sector, more women who own digital skill who can compete to win.

High digital skill occupations more easier than men because employers usually select female to do high skill occupations easier than make. However, if those professional service female employees can not learn how to apply digital skills to do these researchs medical treatmentm architectural design professional service jobs. Then, it is also different for these professional service femal employees to raise competition in global labour professional service market. So, these professional service female employees need to learn how to apply digital to do themselves jobs in future global professional service labour market. Otherwise, if the male professional service employees can attempt to learn how to apply digital skill to do themselves jobs in order to improve efficiencies and service performance to satisfy patients, such as medical service needs, school search service needs, construction firms' building needs. Then, the owning high digital technology skillful female employees will be more easier to find the professional service jobs which need digital skill more easier than the lacking digital skill female service professionals in future global digital service professional labour market.

On the other robotic communication skill need aspect, future employers expect workers to know how to communicate with robots to work efficiently in any working environment if the employers need robotc to serve their organizations. For example, communication between the robots on factory floors, and between people and robots could allow robots to start and stopr processes based on real-time conditions around them and alert people when there is a problem, so robots could increase their own efficiency if the workers could monitor themselves and determine when they needed maintenance; efficiency would also be improved if machines and robots could make production decisions on their own by. For example, ordering new suppliers when existing inputs into a production process run low. The increase in productivity of industrial robots will likely reduce the number of manual jobs on the shop floor.

At the same time, the increased output made possible by such robots will mean that manufacturers need more people in accounting, finance, sales, advertising and other roles. The increase in putput may also drive increased employment on manufacturers' supply chains. Hence, future employers expect to employ the workers who can know how to communicate with robots to work efficiently in order to raise productivity in any working environment. It means that it the worker can know how to control and communicate with the robots to work together in the team. Then, his/her communication and controlling robotic skill will help the organization's team to work efficiently and raise productivity in order to reduce time waste and human waste and resource waste considerately. So, future shortage of communication and controlling robotic skillful workers number will increase. It has much beneficial to workers who choose to attempt to learn how to communicate and control robots to work together in any working environment team efficiently. Because future employers will like to use robots to assist manual workers to attempt to raise productive efficiency in any working environment. So, the need of employees who know how to cooperate or communicate with robots whose talent skills will be useful to any future employers.

Future global business leaders will need human machine cooperation skill. This technological skill includes artificial intelligence (AI and internet of things (IOT), will reshape our working change. These machines will participate to our daily working environment. For instance, many business leaders agree that automated systems will free-up their time as well as they also believe they'll have more job satisfaction by offloading the tasks that they don't want to do to intelligent machines.

Therefore, future leaders will expect humans and machines can work as integrated teams within their organizaton in order to their workforce and machines are already successfully working this way. So, they need to expect future employees can know or learn how to work with automated systems more easily, because many jobs will be participated by automated systems, e..g simple accounting tasks, legal administration tasks etc. clerical tasks. They will be participated with (AI) technology, it learns how to cooperate with (AI) technology to finish simplt clerical tasks efficiently.

Future workers will need have autrmated system operational skills: They include that how to operate automated systems to free -up workers' time. Workers will need to learn how to operate automated system to better with healthcare tracking devices workers will need to learn how to operate automated systems to absord and manage information in completely different ways. Workers will need to learn how to operate automated systems of smart machines to work as admin. in any orking environments. Workers need be needed to learn how to operate (AI) automated machines to mak more accurate clerical tasks or efficiencies. So, the automated system (robotic) operational skillful workers' demand and number will increase.

In the future, employers need automated machine manufacturing and service with workers cooperation reasons include that clear protocols, will need to be established if autonomous machines fail. So, they need their workers to learn how to control and manage and communicate with autonomous machines skillfully. They believe move they depend upon technology, the more they'll have to lose in the event of a cyber attack. So, skillful workers are real required to let them to know how to cooperate with autonomous machines more efficiently and easily. Computers will need to be able to decipher between good and bad commands, so future employers have much chance to need the owning automated machines operating workers to assist any robots to make more accurate good or bad decision when robots and workers have need to make immediate judgement in their any related job responsibilites aspect.

Therefore, future owning automated machines operating workers' skillful level will be high. It bases on automated machine manufacturing environment trend factor. Finally, future technology will connect the right employee to the high task at the right time. It implies that when future global employers began to accept to apply robots to help them to raise any productivities efficiently. It will influence many manufacturing positions which need to employ any proficient skillful workers who own automated machines operational skills to know how to communicate or manage or control , even supervise any robots to work in teams in any organizational manufacturing environment efficiently. In the future, employers also expect employees to own sufficient digital vision and strategic skills, manifest among other things. They can know how to apply data to demonstrate any senior support and sponsorship digital technological skill. They expect to reduce a skill gap and avoid a lack of employee buying and a workforce culture to change in their digital technologicl manufacturing organizations. Future employers also believe outdated technology that can't work fast enough, data overload, privary and security concerns. So, it explains why it is possible that future employers also need digital working environment and automated robots machines to attempt to achieve raising productive efficient aim.

Moreover, it also explains why digital transformation need will be raised. The reasons include: They feel digital technology can gain employees' buying in , making customer experience a boardroom concern, achieving fair compensation , training and goals and strategy achievement more easily, tasking senior leaders with digital working environment change putting policies and technology to support a fully remote, flexible workforce , empowering lines of team work more efficient, teaching all employees how to code/understanding how to adopt to work with automatic machines or rots in any team efficiently. So, automate machine can raise efficiency in manufacturing society.

In conclusion, in the future business society, employees need to be stronger human machine partnerships. So , future manufacturing or service industries will have digital technology and automated machine robotic technology to assist workers to work in any working environment efficiently. They expect digital technology and automated machine robotic technology anticipation to workers' daily jobs in order to bring positive impacting to the customer experience from business owners to decision makers in marketing, customer service, research and developmnt and finance etc. They also expect technological productivity can bring positive relationship between technology and workers emerging technologies' impact on business and the way workers and automated machine work together.

CHAPTER THREE

Economy Theory

Q1 What is time series perspective on economic growth to pursue for growth and human development strategies ?
A time series perspective is explained on economic growth may be more useful to pursue for growth and human development strategies. A time series can allow to pursue time series studies for particular countries or country groups at particular stages of economic growth. It can allow for a more specific micro behavior of economic agents. In general, any country has three income groups, such as low income, lower-middle income and upper middle income groups. Also, any country may have these four types of public expenditure for human development which including: enhancing education and building up of human capital, public investment to finance general market and subsistence production, e.g. transportation system, such as roads, bridges, harbors, water supply, sanitation, health and care and education.

A 2005 year study had been carried by Dimonson, Marsh & Staunton, which performed an analysis is stock returns in 53 countries, going back to 1900 year for 17 countries, did not find evidence of a significant long term positive relationship between GDP growth rates and equity returns. Also the analysis from Schroders Economics team found that over the past sixty years, there has tended to be a positive relationship between GDP growth and equity market returns during the recovery, expansion and slowdown phases of the traditional business cycle. This relationship has traditionally broken down during the recession phase.

The Schroders economics team also indicated a traditional business cycle model, which has four stages. In the beginning, it is slowdown stage. It means output above trend, growth decelerating and inflation rising. Next is recession stage. It means output below trend, growth developing, inflation falling. Then, it is recovery stage. It means output below trend, growth decelerating, inflation falling. Finally, it is expansion stage, it means output above trend growth accelerating, inflation is rising. The economic team also suggested the traditional business cycle model: In the slowdown stage, GDP growth is positive, but falling, inflation is high and rising, so policy strategy is tight recommended in the recession stage, GDP growth is negative and falling, inflation is falling. So, policy strategy is loosening recommended. In the recovery stage, GDP growth is negative and rising, inflation is low and falling, so policy strategy is loose recommended. Finally, the expansion stage, GDP growth is positive and rising, inflation is rising, so policy strategy is tightening recommended.

It seems that governments ought concern the business cycle period to evaluate themselves country GDP growth to achieve the most effective policy to adopt to achieve different human development policies to invest to present economic recession crisis occurrence. Usually, in the recovery and expansion phases of the business cycle, the stock market tends to perform well as rising GDP and earnings growth drives positive excess returns on equity. In the slowdown phase, inflation is still high and monetary policy remains tight, resulting in s difficult environment for corporations. reducing earnings and stock valuations tends to result in negative excess returns for equities: declining GDP growth is therefore usually matched with poor equity performance. It also explained that during the recession phase, there is often GDP growth is falling, but the excess return on equity tends to be positive. Historically, falling inflation and an accompanying loosening of monetary policy is needed to rise re-rating.

Thus, it seems the business cycle and human development policy has close relationship. During in the slowdown stage, GDP growth is positive, but falling, inflation is high and rising, then the country's government ought spend less expenditures to human development because GDP growth is stable growth. Otherwise, during it is recession stage or recovery stage, it means output below trend, growth developing, inflation falling. Then the country's government ought spend more to invest to any human development needs to prepare to raise whose labor productivity and GDP growth. Finally, during the expansion stage, GDP growth is positive and rising, inflation is rising. Then the country's government can spend less expenditures to invest human development. Thus, any country's government ought concern what is whose country's business cycle stage to arrange to spend more or less expenditures to achieve its human development policy in different business cycle stages.

Q2 How to apply quantitative evidence to review policy to improve economic growth ?
Nowadays, political scientists began to apply quantitative methods to classify and measure political interactions. In general, any countries' policies that maximize growth are optimal that cares solely about pure " capitalists". The greater, the inequality of wealth and income, the higher rate of taxation and the lower growth. It shows that inequality in land and income ownership is negatively with subsequent economic growth. Many economists have tried to explain lower growth rates and unemployment with a growing tax burden in many developed countries. Although, the impact of taxes on growth can be observed both from the aspect of efficiency and aspect of changes in equity that taxes introduce to economy.

I shall indicate how to apply quantitative evidence to review policy to improve economic growth. In fact, economic or welfare outcomes to changes in regulatory policy has close relationship to be suggested outcome indicate to reduce risk face economic recession occurrence to any countries. Every country government ought design to gather quantitative data to prepare any policy implementation to support mutual learning and best practice in different societal and market conditions. The goal is to help countries to build better government systems and implement policies at both national and regional level that lead to sustainable economic and social development.

The critical public policy challenge is to ensure that the expected economic benefits from regulatory changes are both achieved and outweigh any economic cost imposed. I shall indicate evidence on the outcomes of regulatory policies to help policymakers how design regulatory measures that work better. This method is called "regulatory management". This regulatory management study suggests some conclusions to any policymakers as below:

● Firstly, poorly designed policy regulation can not raise economic activities and ultimately reduce economic growth.

● Secondly, it is impossible between a regulatory policy change and the impact on economic outcomes, such as economic growth is from statistic method easily.

● Thirdly, the reliance on economic recession analysis to investigate the relationship across countries between regulatory variables and economic outcomes may not be readily applicable to any countries and may not always be expressed in economic values. It is particularly useful in developing countries regulatory policy measures for recommendation to policymakers only.

● Fourthly, most quantitative studies deal with the costs of regulation and give little or no attention to quantifying the benefits of regulation. For the policymaker, it is important to compare the estimated costs of regulation. Any policy regulation is intended to correct market failures and assist to economic efficiency and growth. The public policy aims to reduce socially unacceptable income and wealth distributions or it can satisfy expectation that the public should have access to certain products and services, e.g. health care and education irrespective of ability to pay, such as merit products. Some of regulation, that governments need to concern, e.g. of property rights, company law, law of contract etc. and regulation can provide important economic and social, including environmental benefits.

Of course, those benefits need to be set against the costs. Because regulations are the operations of effective economies and societies to market rules, e.g. law of contract and protecting property rights and the rights of citizens. It seems regulatory management is important to influence any policies can be achieved effectively, due to one good regulation can supervise the leader's behavior and otherwise one bad regulation can not supervise the leader's behavior, even it can not assist the country economic growth for long term. So, any leader needs to concern how to use quantitative evidence to review huaman development policy if who hopes whose policy's regulations are achieved effectively.

Regulatory management method

At the same time, economic, environmental and welfare pressures raise the demand for regulation above minimum needed for operating a market economy to prepare to face the economic recession occurrence. So, evidence on the outcomes of regulatory policies should help policymakers design regulatory measures that work better. Similarly, evidence on the success or failure of regulation can be used for public accountability purposes.

Regulatory policy defines as the process by which government, when identifying a policy objectives, decides whether to use regulation as a policy instrument and proceeds to draft and adopt a regulation through evidence based decision making. The strategy shall commit governments to remain a regulatory management system, articulating regulatory policy goals, and the impacts of regulation on competitiveness and economic growth. For example, regulation, such as employment law or competition law, the regulation of employment law is applied to control any employers' behaviors to give the fair treatment to whose employees and to protect employees' benefits.

Besides the regulation of competition law is applied to control the fair competition in market. Why this regulations has direct relationship to economy growth. An identifiable economy theory of specific regulatory policies, e.g. administrative simplification and specific economic and welfare outcomes, e.g. high economic growth. The result is a series about the impact of regulatory management on economic indicators. There can be set out as a causal. Thus regulation can be supportive of market transactions and may result in significant economic, social and environmental benefits.

At the same time, ill-designed regulation can have appreciable economic costs, leading to the concept of regulatory burden. In particular, good regulation can reduce the chance of lower economic growth or GDP occurrence, damage investment and competitiveness. But, it has also weakness, such as regulatory costs may act as a barrier to entry into industry in the form of set up cost, e.g. installing equipment to meet health and safety laws and on going annual cost, e.g. preparing returns and facilities inspections.

However, regulatory can be unduly costly to comply with administrator and enforce, but it simplification can reduce the regulatory burden. For example, regulation may not only affect the behavior of those targeted by a rule (direct effects), but invoke behavioral change in the economy (indirect effects). Whether regulation can support governments to avoid or reduce the threats of economic recession occurrence, it depends on the leader's concern how to use quantitative evidence to review policy before who decides to implement which kinds of regulatory management methods.

In recent year, some countries had considered how to achieve policy field with a view to introducing better regulation. The aim is to ensure that regulation occurs only when it does improve social welfare and that regulatory changes do, so with the minimum net cost or maximum net benefit to society. For a policy making perspective, it is important to appreciate how and why a regulatory achievement can be expected to result in a particular impact.

Causal chain analysis is a technique for explaining the way in which a caused regulatory results in an economic impact. By helping to understand the how and why questions, regulatory impact, so causal chain analysis can provide policymakers, with relevant information on the consequences of their policy decisions. It seems that regulation can lead economic improvements, such as higher GDP growth, higher productivity, move business start ups. etc. Due to the causal chain analysis relates to each component separately. So, any decision maker hopes to achieve better regulation, who needs time to attempt to different regulations to achieve whose policies every year. Then, who can review why whose policy can not improve whose country's economic growth as well as to attempt to find reasons how to apply better regulatory to achieve better policy to improve its country's economic growth. It seems review regulatory policy which ought to concern to any decision maker, if who wanted to achieve better regulatory policy to raise economic and welfare gains every year.

In capitalism view, capitalism tends equal systematically, through not uniformly to reward business behaviour that is honest, fair civil and compassionate. When does irrational honesty behaviour influence social economy development? It concerns behavioral economy to individual decision maker whose individual psychology, social psychology into economics. It helps policy makers to incentive in market transactions and in response to policy interventions. So, policy advisers are already using the finding of behavioural economy to advantage to public policy, there is nothing about behavioural economy, but for a long time, it has tended to be concerned how the social economic development, particularly in macroeconomy. For example, policy makers concern of money in nominal rather than real terms in whose how to solve to unemployment. Also, policy makers neglect to recognize how economic motivations apart from those based on rational calculation usually. Most, probably of policy decision makers' decisions to will be drawn out over many days to come, who feels action rather than inaction to any decision immediately, and not as the outcome of a weighted average of probabiities. It seems that the policy decision maker's irrational honesty behaviour will influence how our social's economic development to be good or bad.

Q3 How individual tax payable honest behavior influences economic growth ?
Whether it has relationship between political instability and national economic performance. By past history indicated that the depletion of resource during wars may be one reason why some countries fail to sustain adequate economic growth. However, because economic growth affects a population's well being, this question concerning how was related to growth is important from a policy perspective. So, civil wars can influence any country's economic growth because war can cause the falling changes in a country's physical and human capital as well as lacking technology supporting can reduce GDP per capita to be country during war occurs. For example, during war does noe occur, then trade liberalization, democracy, government stability and a legal system that strongly protects private property rights enhance growth.

During the political instability is occurring, whether tax policy can assist economic growth and social welfare growth. On of central questions in macroeconomics and public policy is how changes in tax policy affect economic activity and social welfare. Consequently, it is possible that sometimes, taxing leads to inefficiency in economy. Whether can taxes stimulate people to change their behavior. For example, the person could either work so hard as before introduction of taxes and reduce whose spending, or work more and spend less time at leisure, thus not needing to reduce spending substantially. However, the inefficiency is caused by taxes, will be presented with a simple supply and demand diagram. In other words, taxes have impact on the amount of supply and demand for products and services.

The purpose of understanding of the impact of taxes on welfare, the decrease in welfare of consumers and producers should be compared with the tax revenue by the country. Such an analysis will show that the decrease in consumers' and producers' welfare exceeds the tax revenue collected by the country. The loss of welfare that takes place after introduction of taxes (a part of which belongs to no one either to a consumer or producer, nor to the country) represents a weight loss or excess tax burden as a degree of inefficiency that taxes introduce to economy. However, full understanding of weight loss requires a detailed tax burden of analysis is needed to governments.

What determines the size of the heavy weight loss to tax? A higher price elasticity of demand curve, or a higher price elasticity of supply curve can lead to a higher weight loss to tax. The more elastic the curves are, the higher is the inefficiency that taxes introduce to the market. The fact is taxes introduce heavy weight loss to the economy because which stimulate people to change their behavior. Since elasticity of supply and demand is a measure of change in the behavior of consumers and producers in relation to change of prices , it also determines the rate of market distortion. The more elastic supply and demand curves, the higher is the heavy weight loss. Another important determinant of the size of heavy weight loss is the tax rate. When price elasticity of supply and demand is the same, heavy weight loss is low when taxes are low and it grows when which both grow. Indeed, heavy weight loss grows faster than most taxes: we can sat that the size of heavy weight loss provided that production costs are constant is equal to 1/2 (elasticity / product quantity), where it is tax rate. Elasticity is price elasticity of demands, product is price of Q is quantity of products.

Individual tax payable honest behavior influences economic growth

What is taxation of savings and investment relationship? Taxes can reduce economic growth by affecting savings and investment. The higher the proportion of income that is being saved and invested, the higher will be the future income level, In other words, through its impact on the amount of the income being saved or invested, taxation policy has a crucial effect on the future level of income per capita. The impact of taxes on saving of individuals and companies, investment in fixed capital and investment risk is briefed represented below: How impact of taxes on savings of individual? The gross savings in private sector and accumulated in households and companies.

However, a large past of the gross savings is used for covering depreciation and is needed for the existing capital. The net savings, consisting of savings to householders and earnings of companies, represent the real potential, available for new investments. If all householders would save the same proportion of income, then the impact of income tax on the total savings would be the same, regardless of the pattern of the distribution of tax burden to individuals. But, wealthy individuals shall save more than poor citizens. So, it is expected that the tax collected from higher tax brackets create more burden on savings than the ones collected from lower tax brackets.

Consequently, on individual tax behavior view, a more progressive income tax seems to be creating a heavier burden on savings than a less progressive tax system. So I suggest a less progressive income tax policy will encourage more savings of individuals. However, it is a only assumption, it has another factors to influence citizen's tax behavior: such as, a varies during a life cycle in youth and in old age, it is much lower saving than in middle are when income in highest and when people save for education of their children for a house or flat and for the old age to prepare retirement. So, tax policy is not considered by firms or policymakers in isolation from other aspects of site selection including benefits from public products which are needed to use by citizens, e.g. gardens, swimming pools, entertainment facilities etc. different public facilities.

Finally, I shall explain why individual tax payable honest behavior has moral consequences to cause economic growth. For citizens of all too many of the different countries, where poverty is still the normal. But the tangible improvements in the basic of life that make economic growth, so important whenever living standards are low, greater life expectancy, few diseases, less infant mortality and malnutrition have mostly been played out long before a country's per capita income reaches the levels enjoyed in today's advanced industralized economy.

In fact, immoral or dishonesty business or economic behaviours are caused by some people who pursue material well being and who aim to do benefit to themselves, but it will cause illegal money transactions to raise any overall country's economic or GDP growth. In fact, this business transactions are not legal. So, which can't cause GDP or economic growth to any country. Also, the illegal businesses can not contribute any benefits to any society, so which can not bring any economic benefits or welfares to any countries to satisfy any citizen'e needs ensurely. Even, in parts of the world where the need to improve nutrition and literacy and human life expectancy is urgent, there is often aspect to the recognition that achieving superior growth is a top priority. So, it seems dishonesty behaviours will not improve and raise low income level people whose life expectancy and life quality because this illegal businesses income is used to spend to the illegal businesses or immoral policy decision makers themselves benefits and who won't spend to social welfare.

It seems that these illegal businesss or immoral policies can not assist any economic growth and raise GDP growth rate as well as dishonesty or immoral economic activities can not bring any benefits to societies in our world, even these bad behaviours will bring harm to our societies. e.g. encouraging illegal drug sale to harm young people health and raising crimes rates; winning illegal gamble to earn illegal profit to increase high interest loan businesses and crimes or causing bad families relationship to raise social challenges.

What is the root of the irrational behavioural problem? I believe that is our conventional thinking about economic growth fails to reflect the breadth of what growth, or its absence, means for any society. There are some people's dishonest behaviours only weigh material positives against moral negatives. I believe this dishonest economic activites are seriously. In some cirsumstances dangerous incomplete, the value of arising standard of living lies individuals live, but in how it shapes the social, political and ultimately the moral character of a people.

Economic growth means a rising standard of living for the clear majority of citizens. So, dishonest economic behaviours can only give benefits to the individual and these irrational behaviours can not give welfare to overall societies. In fact, economic growth bears moral benefits as well. So, it seems dishonest behaviours can not raise moral benefit, then it can not also raise economic growth to any country. Moreover, dishonest behaviours are also caused to any country's political democracy. e.g. Many policy decision makers usually only consider self benefit, so who will neglect to consider social welfare benefits to whose citizen. Themselve benefit behaviours will be unfair to whose citizen. The importance of the connection between economic growth and social and political progress and the consequent concern for what will happen of living standards tail to improve, are not limited to the United States and other countries that already have high income and established democracies. So, economic growth or its absence often plays a significant role not only progress from dictatorship to democracy, but also the democracies by new dictatorships.

Also, for dishonest behaviours are caused by decision makers, such as the link between economic growth and social and political progress in the developing countries has yet other political implicatons as well. For example, the continuing absence of political demoracy and basic personal freedoms in China has deeply troubled many observers in the West. Until China gained admisson to the World trade Organization in 2002 year, these concerns regularly gave rise in the Uniter States to debate on whether to trade with China on a most favored nation basis. These concerns still cause questions about whether to give Chinese firms advantage advanced American oil company. Both sides in this debate share the same objective: to foster China's political liberalization. How to do so , however, remains the focus of intense disagreement. The improvement in nutrition, housing, sanitation and transportation has been dramatic, when the freedom of Chinese citizens to make economic choices, where to work, what to buy, when to start a business is already broader than it was with continued economic advance, the average Chinese standard of living is still only one eighth that in the United states, greater freedom to make political choices too, it will probably follow. So the economy is actually developing, like China won't have to wait until China can achieve Western level incomes before they experience significant political and social liberalization.

To conclude, if any country's policy makers who do not consider citizen welfare and who only consider self benefit, it will cause dishonest behaviours to influence social economic development to cause poor situation for long term. So, policy makers must need concern their behaviors are rational choice to make any economic decisions to let their citizen to give welfares for long term. Also any businessmen ought choose to do rational economic behaviours to benefits for societies and clients and governments in order to achieve economic growth to GDP to their countries if who hope whose businesses can be stable to compete for long term. So, policy decision makers and businesses ought consider rational honesty behaviour before who do any economic decision.

Q4 How does every country government teach its citizen to do social moral honest behavior which can brings economic growth?

How honesty is influenced to economic positive relationship. The dishonesty behaviour includes: e.g. corruption is as an illegal payment to a public agent to obtain a benefit that may or may not be deserved, or the abuse of public office for private gains to consume, corruption probably amounts are to a large share of the gross national product in any countries. So, corruption worries policy makers and international organizations, who remains the adverse effects of corruption.

However, in the macroeconomic view, the academic literature is less definite about how bribes minimize the waiting costs associated with queuing in a equilibrium. Both of those waiting cost associated with queuing and inefficiency models equate bribes as allocating the true worth of the licenses or permit to the most worthy bidder in public sector. Forbidding bribes that amounts to prohibiting the use of price mechanism in the public sector. In terms of economic growth, the only thing worse than a society over centralized, dishonest bureaucracy is over-centralized. So, the quality of government institutions, including the degree of corruption, affects investment and growth as much as other political economy variable. e.g. political freedom, civil liberties and political violence. Another example, some firms that pay more bribes also spend more time with bureaucrats in more corrupt countries and have a higher cost of capital, thus countering the view of corruption.

Some countries are likely fairer and regulation is less. How does corruption affect income inequality? In addition, capital market imperfection and government spending have been suggested as two channels for corruption to affect inequality and economic growth. Finally, to what extent can corruption explain the differences in inequality and economic growth? So, it seems corruption is associated with a smaller increase in income inequality and a larger drop in growth rates. Also, corruption raises income inequality to a lesser extent in countries to achieve higher government spending. So, it seems corruption dishonest behaviour has close relationship to influence any countries' GDP economic growth.

Corruption is understood as sale of government property for private gain. However, most economists view corruption as a major obstacle to development. It is seen as one of the causes of low income and is believed to play a critical role in poverty. Perhaps the most quoted example of this is speed money paid by business people to government officials to speed up bureaucraties procedures. At the macro level, there is evidence that corruption affects adversely many of the proxy causes of economic growth. e.g. investment in manufactured and human capital. Moreover, high levels of corruption tend to with a lack of political accountability and disrespect for property rights factors which themselves tend to be obstacles to economic growth.

More fundamentally, however, there is a sense in which the focus on growth in GDP per capita is misguided. Ultimately, development is about how to improvement in human welfare. However, corruption is developing a few with access systematic distort political and economic decisions which might be made systematically with conflict of interest at play. For example, different countries' banks which achieve different bank schemes to aim to avoid illegal money saving from drug trafficking to cause false economic growth in any countries. The anti-corruption strategy advocated to economic development, democratic reform a strong civil society with access to information and overseeing the state, and the presence of rule of law. The governance program facilities at the request of client governments, a series and surveys involving broad segments of society and national and local government performance.

The causes of its development and many and vary from one country to the next. It seems corruption dishonest behaviours can cause to seem as one country's false economy growth and even, global false economy growth after any illegal economic activities had been done from any illegal businessmen. So corruption is a global issue which is government all over the world. However, what is the causes and consequences of corruption? It is possible that corruption is the intentional with length relationship aimed at deriving some advantage from this behaviour for oneself or for related individuals. So, in micro-economic view, corruption cause is derived from some advantage from this behaviour for the person. Otherwise, in macro-economic view, corruption cause is also derived from some advantage this behaviour for the organization, even overall country's social benefit, e.g. illegal shares buying and selling trading activities, illegal bank saving transaction source from drug trafficking activities.

On citizen educational honest behavior aspect, many of the assumptions which are attempted to rationalize the process of educational development have been criticized or abandon. However, the education quality role of different educational regulation, the choice of financing methods, the examination and certification procedures or various other regulation and incentive structures will influence educational effect to satisfy public needs. Thus, citizen honest educational policy makers need to satisfy public needs. Moreover, educational policymakers also need to concern any new policy making environment which will seriously constrain their attempts to ensure the early discussion of planning considerations as part of the education policy making process. So, every country's environment factor will influence every educational policymaker's individual decision.

As defined, policy represents decisions that are designed to guide (including to constrain future decisions or to initiate and guide the implementation of previous decisions). It is this time bound nature of policy and of policy making that makes it is such a critical concern for the educational planner. However, the failure of the traditional planning models and the recognition of the lack of nationality that can occur in policy making there combined to create an atmosphere of pessimism among some educationalists.

To capture the details of the decision making process of any educational planning itself, an analytical framework is presented that goes beyond the initial decision point to examine both the preceding actions (contextual assessment, technical analysis and the generation, valuation and selection of policy options) and the subsequent activities (planning and conducting implementation, impact assessment and where appropriate, design). Thus, the framework covers the full policy planning process, but with a focus on the facilitating and constraining effects that policy decisions and how they were derived and have no the choices available to citizen honest educational planners.

There are two ways of value to educational planners. First, the methodology of the framework and conclusions of the any one of educational case studies should help in the analysis of current educational policies and decision making procedures (an analysis of policy). So, it is a present method to gather current data from current case studies to make the update conclusions to achieve any any of eductional policies. Otherwise, Second, the another framework can be applied to have evaluation of proposed policies and used to forecast policy outcomes and the probability of successful implementation, given the country of fiscal and management capacity, political commitment etc. So, this framwork is a futuer predict educational method to gather data how to get the recommedation to achieve the effiective quality of educational policy in the future.

Citizen honest behavioral sducational policy can be lower differ in terms of scope, complexity, decision environment, range of choices and decision criteria. Any educational policy decision deals with large scale policies and broad resource allocation will have these questions to need to answer. For example, on strategic view, how can we provide basic education at a reasonable cost to meet equity and efficiency objectives?

On multi program view, should resources be allocated to university level education? On program view, how would occupational training centre be designed and provided across the country? On issue specific view, should graduated of rural universities be allowed to transfer to any one of city area universities to study easily? On the psychological view, some researches indicated behavioral economics with emotions has close relationship to any policy making, such as educational policy. More recently, economists as well as psychologists who are specifically interested in decision making have begun to take greater concerning emotional influence.

So, it seems any policy decision making whose any one of final policy decisions which is influenced to achieve or not achieve from their emotion indirectly. Usually, then an economy is doing well, there is less incentive to encourage new entrepreneurial firms if the country's citizens and firms have enough jobs supply and have enough labor supply in the job market. It seems that good economic growth country will have this question why it needs to take a risk on something new. So, emotions have close link to our societies to influence any country's citizens real needs and entrepreneurs' business aim to develop any societies' economy to be grown. So, any countries' policies decision makers ought concern whose enterprises and citizens whose real needs, then who can attempt to choose what methods of policies to assist whose countries' economy development more effective.

Q5 How can natural environment protection policy influence economy growth ?

On natural environment protection policy, whether national environment protection policy can assist economic growth to the country. The natural environment is central to economic activity and growth, providing the resources, we need to produce products and services and absorbing and processing unwanted by-product in the form of pollution add waste. So, environment assets contribute to managing risks to economic and social activity helps to regulate flood risks, regulating the local climate both air quality and temperature and maintaining the supply of clean water and resources both.

Government's environment protection role is to send clear signals and set a long term policy framework in order to provide businesses with the certainty who need to make investments in low carbon and resource efficient technologies. It is also essential that government listens to and works with business, so that environment protection policies are designed in a way that avoids unnecessary burdens and removes potential barriers to success. So, the natural environment plays an important role in supporting economic activity. It contributes: directly, by providing resources and raw materials, such as water, timber and minerals that are required as inputs for the production of products and services and indirectly, through services provided by ecosystems including carbon water purification, managing flood risks and nutrient cycling.

The relationship between economic growth and the natural environment is complex. Several different drivers come into play, including the scale and composition of the economy, particularly the share of services in GDP as opposed to primary industries and manufacturing and changes in technology that have the potential to reduce the environmental impacts of production and consumption decisions when also driving economic growth.

In fact, economic growth involves the combinations of different types of capital to produce products and services these include; produced capital, such as machinery, buildings and roads; human capital, such as skills and knowledge, natural capital, e.g. raw materials are extract from the earth, carbon and services is provided by forests and social capital, such as institutions and ties within communities. So, government needs to concern that national resources can not be extracted too much to lead our natural capital is lacked to produce any products or to provide services in the future.

In particular, market failure in the provision and use of environmental resources mean that natural assets would be over-used in the absence of government intervention. These market failures arise from the public product characteristics of the natural environment, external costs and benefits, where the use of a resource by one party has impacts on others, difficulties in capturing the full benefits of business investment in environmental research and development, and information failure. Market failures may include water quality and to vehicle emissions to influence human's body health.

So I suggest that any countries' government needs to achieve these policies which concerns on environmental protection aspect to achieve its public spending and technology policy, such as below:

● On developing flood infrastructure hand, supporting low carbon technologies electric vehicles. Also on the information provision and other policies to address barriers to influence consumer's behavior change, such as product labelling policies and policies to increase take up of resource efficiency measures to provide environment protection. So, effective environmental policy is likely to require and the use of multiple instruments, each tackling to require part of the problem when avoiding duplication and unnecessary regulatory burdens. Also, pricing environmental inputs can correctly help any businessmen to manage how to use natural resources effectively.

● Environmental policy aims to reduce how the economy and the businesses are to adverse environmental events, by reducing environmental risk both. For example, not just investments that facilities emissions reductions to avoid dangerous climate change, but also those investments that help to economy adapt to climate impacts already locked in by past and current emissions. The natural environment plays a key role in our economy, as a direct input into production and through the many services it provides. Environmental resources, such as minerals and fossil fuels directly facilities the production of products and services. The environment provides other services that enable economic activity, such as carbon, filtering air and soil formation. It is also vital for against flood risk, and soil formation. It is also vital for our wellbeing, providing us with recreational opportunities, improving our health and much more. Human wellbeing in a complex and diverse concept, determined by a wide-range of factors including levels of income absolute and relative, health status, educational attainment, housing conditions and environmental quality.

● National capital contributes to economic output through two main channels: directly as an input to the process of economic activity, indirectly through its effect on the productivity of the other factors of production. However, natural capital is as a direct input to wealth creation, which can provide the raw materials for economic production of products the raw materials for economic production of products and services, it includes non renewable resources like, fossil fuels, minerals metal extracted from the natural environment to produce energy, machinery, consumer products, renewable resources, natural processes or own reproduction. Why do our governments need to concern environmental policy? The reasons include natural areas provide global life support functions, including climate regulation and regulation of the chemical composition of the atmosphere and oceans. When natural areas play a role in the maintenance of life essential services, it is difficult to evaluate and demonstrate the contribution that particular habitat types or areas make. Water regulation can reduce flood and storm protection and prevent damage. Natural processes can also provide water quality benefits, pollution includes the removal of nutrients and pollutants from water, filtering of dust from the air, and providing noise. Waste sink includes all non recycled waste is produced by economic activity. In the absorptive capacity of the atmosphere, the oceans and the soil protection, such as many wetland habitats, provides benefits by preventing soil loss. Nutrient cycling includes storage, processing and acquisition of nutrients essential for plant growth in ecological process and waste decomposition, naturally occurring micro-organisms provide benefits through their ability to break down organization matter and speed up the process of waste decomposition.

Q6 How financial crisis influences economy growth ?

As the global financial crisis has reminded as once again of the economic role of trust and confidence, social capital attributes which are difficult to influence any policy decision maker's ration decision making more easily. Referring to recent financial crisis, which is related to any psychological drivers of economy activity, we can not understand the economic developments of recent times without psychological insights which go beyond estabished notions of rationality in its economic sense. As people with weigh the costs and benefits of each possibility.

This above assumption is based on the expectation that individuals and firms will act in a consistent manner, with a reasonably well defined notion of what who like and what whose objectives are, and with a reasonable understanding of how to attain those objectives. In fact, behavioural economy is a complement to deductive processes based on those assumptions. In any discipline with practical applications, such as public policy, conclusion is reached by chains of deductive logic based on those assumptions require the test of falsifiability or refutability, or at least that they be supported by confirmatory evidence. However, a rational means the predictive validity of the rational model holds, but that doesn't mean achieving policy should ignore interventions. For example, most people rationally avoid self-harm, but there will be extreme tails of highly protective and of highly reckless behaviour: the latter may require specific protection. So, it seems it has relationship between global financial crisis and individual or organization's irrational behaviour.

How can government' capturing private investment assist economic growth? How can government's capturing private investment policy attract foreign direct investment or different countries? I believe that Increased levels of trade and foreign direct investment worldwide which has a cause or effect of relationship to the closer interdependence of world economies, they are a reality. What is the relationship among these private, public and civil society sectors? Every country contribution is to add to the public policy stream to understand how the main forces in society operate and cooperate in promoting foreign direct investment. Governments have always been concerned about how to position themselves in an increasingly competitive market for a limited supply of investment resources.

Why should a multi-national firm choose one country attraction ? e.g. tax breaks, profit repatriation, low domestic content requirement etc. How can one country strategically position itself against others? Is there an association between pro-social public policy and levels of global private investment? We are particularly interested in those economies in earlier stages of development, where pro-social policies are a rarer phenomenon, as they provide a testing for our hypotheses. What is the relationship between the ability of an host country to attract private investment and the quality of pubic policies affecting the life of its citizens? Are pro-social host government policies in host countries linked to higher inward flows of foreign direct investment to that country?

There has three country level macroeconomic indicators to represent different facets of size: Host country economy growth rate, host country population and host country's rate of inflation. GDP growth, the annual percent change of output in real terms percent, reflects the strength of local economy and the increase in the size of domestic market, opening the door to large sales and high profits. Thus, higher GDP growth should generally be attracted to larger foreign investment. Population is another indicator of market size. It attracted to foreign investment with both large populations and high GDP per capita. So, encouraging immigration and birth rate can attract more foreign investment. Inflation enters the regression as a proxy for macroeconomic stability and as a reflection of the internal or external shocks suffered by the economy during the period under study, which may attract potential inflation sign of internal economic instability and of the host government's inability to maintain consistent monetary policy. It will influence foreign investment confidence. So stable inflation of the host country can increase confidence to let more foreign investment.

How Capturing private investment policy can affect medium to long term economic growth. It is difficult to measure the factors and to determine causality with certainty, between fiscal policy and economic growth relationship. Fiscal reforms are needed to concern structural reforms, e.g. labor or trade and supportive macroeconomic policies. At the macro level, fiscal policy can help to ensure macroeconomic stability, an essential prerequisite for growth at the micro level, tax and expenditure policies can boost growth by altering work and investment incentives, promoting human capital accumulation and enhancing total factor productivity. For example, combining fiscal reforms, e.g. sealing up infrastructure investment when improving the public investment process can increase their effectiveness. Complementary reforms, such as liberalizing trade of fiscal reforms by promoting savings, stimulating investment and not lacking productivity gains, policy uncertainty and high levels of public debt large fiscal deficits reduce aggregate savings in the economy and may lead to inflation, high interest rates and balance of payments pressures, with negative growth consequences. Policymakers need to concern the durability and equity. For example, Netherland, an expenditure cut of 15% of GDP between 1982 year and 2000 year created room sector job-creation. At the same time, both countries managed to avert adverse consequence on income inequality. In advanced and emerging market economies, age related spending on public persons and health care accounts for a large share of government spending (40% and 30%, respectively, IMF, 2014 f). Otherwise, Poland shifted from a financially defined benefit system to an actuarially solvent defined contribution system, and Germany put its pension system on a more sound financial by linking pension benefits to the old age dependency ratio, tightening access to early retirement and rising the statutory retirement age. In health care, Germany and the Netherlands introduced a combination of macro and micro level reforms to contain cost and enhance efficiency, including price controls on pharmaceuticals, higher co-payment and contributions and budget.

Q7 Can national leadership and economic growth has close relationship? Can leader individual behavior affect economic growth?

Leaders have strongest effects in autocracies, where who appear to substantially influence both economic growth and the evolution of political institutions. I shall indicate to explain why substantial roles for individual leaders and national institutional change, which can further influence the growth environment. In the past, examinations of the fundamental causes of growth debate between institutions, culture and geography, which typically operate without reference to the actions of particular personalities. However, economists may imagine leaders indirectly as policymakers, leaders, themselves are rarely the subject of focus.

The constraints imposed on leaders from electoral pressures, opposition parties, independent legislatures and judiciaries all vary across countries. To the extent that the authority embedded in formal institutional rules and the authority embedded in individuals act as substitutes, the increasing visibility of institutional variation in explaining paths may indirectly motivate leaders' behaviors. Theories of economic growth that emphasize public products, e.g. education, health, public entertainment facilities, such as parks, swimming pools etc. Also, national policies include international trade, monetary policy and fiscal policy etc. or all suggest possibly important roles for a national leader. However, identifying a causative effect of leaders on economic growth is challenging. Even, if it has relationship between particular leaders and particular economic growth in particular economic environment. However, it may be that growth changes drive leadership changes, without a causative effect of leaders. Assumption that a leader quality is independently, it seems the leader has no influence on economic growth. An important additional assumption is that the leader effects are strongest in autocratic settings, especially in the absence of political parties or legislatures to support the leader's any personal view points to achieve any regulations to influence economic growth effectively. These results point to an important effect between institutions and leader individuals in understanding economic growth paths. However, it seems institutions can influence the impact of national leaders behaviors and that national leaders can also influence the path of institutions. If leaders can influence economic growth, then may further these questions are raised: Do leaders act to obstruct economic growth or do they actively promote it? In this view, leaders can be actively good for economic growth, e.g. by investing in public products, choosing pro-growth trade policies, or overcoming national scale coordination problems. However, related questions of how leaders influence growth are related to the role of national policies in explaining growth. If policies might be well matter, even if leaders do not, if national policies care the expression of broader social forces. So, it seems national policies can also influence economic growth, instead of the leader's personal quality. So, it can get this question and conclusion. When asking how do we make poor countries rich? The unexplained, non-deterministic past of economic growth variation becomes especially relevant and given the results about leadership, more within reach.

However, nation leader's behaviour can influence the country's economy development. Concerning irrational honesty whether this behavior can influence social economic development. I shall indicate those questions to attempt to be considered, such as: Can there be a growing scaraity without a growing shortage or a growing shortage with a growing scarcity? Can a decision be economic if there is no money in involved? Can there be surplus food in a society where people are hungry? For example, building ordinary and building luxury housing both involves using many of the same resources, such as bricks, pipes, and construction labour. How does the allocation of these resources between ordinary housing and luxury housing tend to change after rent control laws are passed?

When a government institution or program produces counter productive results, is that necessarily a sign of irrationality on the part of those who run that particular institution or program? Why do American manufacturers of computers or television sets tend to have them transported by others? When Chinese manufacturers tend to transport themselves? How did the movement of population from rural to urban America affect the economy of retail selling in the early twentieth century? Advertising even when it is successful, is often considered to be a benefit only to those who advertise, but of no benefit to consumers, who have to pay the cost of the advertisement in the higher price of the products who buy. Is it irrational economy behaviour to society? Why would luxury hotels be charging lower rates than economy hotels? Whether governments choose to protect competition or protect competitors which method is better? What have been some of the economic and social consequences of the substitution of machine power for human strength, as a result of industralization and the growing importance of knowledge, skills and experience in a high-technological economy? How can per capita income be increasing by 50 % over a period of years, when average family income and average householder income remain almost stable over those same year? Does inequality of income tend to be greater or less in long run than in the short run?

All above questions concern the social and economic influences won't be better if the policy decision makers or businessmen do any irrational honesty behaviours. It seems rational honesty behaviour is important to any policy decision makers or businessmen because whose rational or irrational behaviour can influence social economic development directly are driven to act by economic as well as social ethical and other reasons. So economists need to study of what motivates individual acts, especically regarding economic decisions, offers an intellectual challenge to the human sciences. So, if economists can predict to judge whether any policy decision makers or businessmen whose act is irrational or rational, then who can assist the country's economic development more easily.

Promoting honesty in negotiation can influence social economy growth in global. In a competitive and moral imperfect world, business people are often facing with serious ethical challenges. Usually, many businessmen feel justified in engaging in less than ideal conduct to protect their own interests. However, our commonplace that work to promote credibility, trust and honesty of behaviours can influence our social economy growth in long term. For example, deception in negotiation behaviour is immoral, due to success in business typically requires successful negotiations.

Given the high value placed on honesty, the incentives for deception in negotiation create a serious moral tension for business people. Not surprisingly, deception in negotiation is a widely discussed problem in business ethics. How many negotiators their views are essentially, who is regarded as a superior moral philosopher, would find them objectionable? For example, philosophical debates about the loss of civilian life in war would be better served by putting resources and intellectual energy into developing political, economic diplomatic and military strategies that resources and intellectual energy how to be chosen to use in military strategies aspect or political aspect or economic diplomatic aspect. The country's leader will influence the whole country's social economy development in long term. However, individual and social stability are difficult to maintain in a social setting in which there is serious conflict between ethics and personal welfares. Because irrational honesty behaviour is usually caused between the personal welfare and ethics choice.

Can behavioral economy be applied to develop policy and influence economic growth effectively? Such policies stress that changing the way choices are presented or changing the environment in which decisions are made, can substantially alter behavior. Ideas from behavioral economics have helped to develop the traditional economic choice framework, in which people are assumed to make choices that are rational, self interested and consistent. Some of the most important behavioral insights for tax and benefit policy include: Faced with complicated decisions, people may make choices, which are often approximately optimal, in that who maximize welfare, but might in some cases lead to poor choices. There is evidence that how choices are presented affects outcomes.

The environment in which decisions are made would provide cues to make particular choices or made could provide cues to make particular choices, or some aspects of the choice problem may be more or less influence to consumers. When any policy relates to income and spending, or it is label money for another can affect what people choose to do with it. Individuals appear to care not just about their own outcomes, but also about those of others. This might be because people derive value from fairness and cooperation. These motivations could give intrinsic incentive to make particular choices. It is possible that providing extrinsic incentives, such as taxes, fines or rewards could be crowded our desirable behavior.

Consumers may have to exercise costly self control to make certain choices, such as eating health foods or giving up smoking. Commitment devices to help overcome self control problems are therefore values, for example, raising the cost of tempting choices, increasing cigarette taxes, say: when making choices with uncertain outcomes, people will do a number of behavioral features. Such as, attaching subjective decision weights to each outcome and these may differ from objective measures of probability. Usually, outcomes are measured against a reference point, relative to the reference point are felt more strongly than equivalent gains. When welfare increases and ever bigger gains falls, as the welfare cost is from ever bigger losses, then people will appear to be risk seekers when welfare cost comes to cause social loss. How people value the future changes with the passage of time. Usually people hope to earn immediate rewards in present than distant rewards in the future. This means that people make plans who find it hard to achieve. People may also make choices under the assumption that their preferences won't change in the future. So, for policymakers those biases have important implications for why behavior change interventions may be necessary.

Behavioral insights provide new reasons to intervene, issues of self control, for example, making failure, where outcomes are come from the perspective of either individuals or society or both usually. As a common failure is the case of externalities, when individual choices generate costs or benefits for others. Since, these are not taken into account in private decision making, which are come from a social perspective, there is too much or too little of the activity.

In this case, taxes or subsidies can help private and social incentives. So, behavioral economical concept can be suggested these important insights for externalities, such as private decisions are closer to the social optimum, reducing the need for correcting taxes or subsidies. It seems that taxes or subsidies will affect to change people's behaviors if social preferences are important. Externalities can arise not just because of how someone affects the well being of others, but also through how decisions made today affect the individual in the future. This is known as an internality. Taxes or subsidies policies both can influence people's present behaviors to be changed and future behaviors will be influenced to be changed from whose present behaviors in societies. Thus, policymakers can not neglect this policy of method to attempt to solve any social challenge nowadays.

Finally, I shall explain why national leader's behavior can assist policy development. Behavioral economy is a science, includes psychology, economics, finance and sociology to understand human behavior and decision making. Behavioral economics recognizes that constraints in time and mental resources prevent us from optimally evaluating every decision. To deal with our limitations, so we rely on mental decision to judge our face of uncertainty, but we can be leaded to predictably irrational behaviors from behavioral economical concept.

As government agencies enact laws and regulations that are focused in the society. They often rely on restrictions, incentives or public information campaigns in order to change citizen behavior. When well intentioned, those traditional approaches can be accepted. For example, regulations that can be supported to financial advisers disclose conflicts of interest have led to achieve any final results. Disclosures can increase pressures on advisees to comply with the advice provided and in some cases increase greater perceptions of trust rather than the evaluation of biased advice. Similarly, tax incentives can increase retirement savings rates which have had limited impact. Researchers studying the impact of concluded that such policies are an expensive way of encouraging new savings.

On the one hand, governments ought engage their citizens to do any action, whose action is influenced by behavioral economics to discover how behavioral economics can be provided powerful insights into human motivation and behavior. As different countries' government experiments are more from academic laboratories to the real world. So, it is a kind of method to be applied to assist any countries' governments how to use effective policy to improve people's lives. For example, designing what is the best reasonable taxes, subsidies, incentives or educational campaigns level at the rate, donations and retirement savings rates as well as healthy food product label consumption of selection etc. strategic policies which are related how to apply behavioral economy to analyze or experiment to gain the better choice among of them.

On the another hand, Economic agents ought attempt to spend time to gather data to choose to do the best decision, but not perfectly national ones. Also economic research should be used reasonable assumptions about agents' cognitive actives. So, economic models should take predictions that are consistent with micro-level data on decisions, including experimental evidence. Moreover, economists ought spend much time to learn from psychologists. Behavioral economists now routinely combine experimental data, field data and theory to construct their arguments. As behavioral economic continues to gain acceptance, behavioral economists will increasingly find themselves participating in policy discussions. As policy has the ability to do good or to create great mislead, depending on who, leader is in charge of making the rules. Indeed in some cases the findings of behavioral economists suggest that active policies may be quite harmful. Successful policy analysis should be concerned the motives of private actors, e.g. consumers and firms and the public or governmental actors need to design formulate and enforce policy with cooperation to regulators, bureaucrats, politicians.

So, policy analysis must also be carefully concerned the institutional environment in which these private and public actors interact, e.g. , market, elections and bureaucracies. However, any bad decision making is caused from bounded rationality, slow learning, framing and lack of self control with those effects in mind, one might conclude that government can easily improve consumers' welfare by paternalistically helping consumers make better decisions. Such paternalistic policies can improve consumer welfare by enhancing an individual's maximizing whose own welfare. So, this stands in contrast to most public policies, which address externalities or public products problems that arise because of interactions among economic agents.

To conclude, national leader and whose psychology which can influence whether he can do the reasonable policy and which have close relationship, As if the national leader had health psychology, then who will have more possible to achieve good behavior to perform to decide how to achieve any the best public policies to raise growth to make welfare to whose citizens. So any policymakers ought need to concern how to listen to behavioral scientists to let them to give any recommendation how to improve or review or revise whose psychological challenges to let them have more effort to decide how to choose to do the right decision effectively. Because the relationship between psychology and behavioral science has more generally to influence public policy which is particularly painful and frustrating of the success for any similar policy recommendations. Hence, economics and psychology indeed can provide policymakers with vital tools to develop the best policy to solve any social challenges.

Consequently, it seems the leader's psychology will influence whose behavioral performance to be decided to choose to do the more correct policy to influence economic development more easily. It also means that one leader's psychology is an important factor to influence any social economic development directly for long term. So who can not neglect to concern whether whose psychological mind is right or wrong to already to make any decisions to plan any policies before whose any polices are implemented. Because the leader's psychology will influence whose behavior is more correct to decide to decide how to do any policies effectively.

Reference

Dimson, Marsh & Staunton, London Business School (2005) In The Global Investment Returns Year Book, ABN Amro.

Fiscal Policy And Long Term Growth, International Monetary Fund, IMF policy papers, Washington, D.C. Available from April, 2015, http://www.imf.org/external/pp/ppindex.aspx.

Reference

Abrahamson, E., & Rosenkopf., (1993). Institutional and competitive bandwagons: Using mathematical modeling and a tool to explore innovation diffusion. Academy of management review, 18(3), 487-517.

Hill, C.W.L. & Jones, G.R. 1995. Strategic management, An integrated approach. Boston: Houghtom Mif In.

Q8 Why do future labours need to learn worldwide readiness skills ?

Future employers need employees own worldwide readiness skills, such as reading , writing and arithmatic. Why do employees need worldwide readiness skills? In the future, high economic growth countries need high wage positions, high opportunity jobs which need a large number of skills required of job candidates of these positions " job readinss" and not " job training" , which support developments of these importance and widely desired skills won't only support the success to high-opportunity positions, but also be developed for future success in the competitive global economy. Because real-time business intelligence is needed for the talent marketplace to employ talent employees. So, it explains that it will have many future employers hope to employ owning readiness skillful employees to help them to develop their businesse intelligently. Hence, present employees ought need to hard to train readiness skills to prepare whose future employers' job requirements in the future competitive global job market.

Why these occupations need readiness skills

In the future these occupations will need to raise readiness skills. For example, mathematical science, teachers (post-secondary), management analysts, computer and information systems, managers, first-line supervisors of construction traders, solar photovoltaic installers. All of these occupations , employers need staffs to own good readiness analytic ability to help them to do more accurate real-time business intelligent decisions. The representative occupations include oral and written communication skills, project management, teamwork, marketing and creativity . Moreover, they need to own specific technology skill, deep science and math or even most business skills as well as these skills are "soft" skills more than hard skills. These kinds of occupation employees need own cooperative effort, creativity, problem solving, detail orientation and integrity personal characteristics, which are relevant across all knowledge and domains.

Therefore, in the future, science, technology,engineering and mathematics relevant occupations need to own more readniness and analytic skills more than othe kinds of occupations. Because these organizations need those professionals on knowledge acquisition, literacy analysis, synthesis and critical thinking skills that will impact their organizations to bring more critical thinking beneficial team culture. These occupational top skills will include oral and written communication skills, project management skill, team oriented skill, marketing and creativity skills, problem solving skill, detail oriented skill, self-motivated skills, management and analytical skills, coaching skill, business process modeling skills, work independent skill, strong leadership skills, management experience and business requirements gathering. All of these skills which will be future employers who need to employ these kinds employees who own these skills in preference. Also, all of these skills concentrate on soft skills more than hard skills. It seems that when above occupational applicants who own any one of thes skills, evn more than one skills. Then, he/ she will have more chance to be selected to employ. Also occupation specific skills requirements are more needed to compare cross-functional skills for above of any one occupation. Because the high concentraton of cross-functional skills require " job readiness" and not " job training" for success, e.g. communicaton, integraton and presentation skills, entrepreneurialism and related skills, microsoft office software skills.

Of particular interest is communication, integration and presentation skills. These skills include ability to seek, evaluate and examine information and data create a reasoned position, present findings and make a case for or advocate for position. So, these skills are very important and they can help future applicants who expect to win any kinds of these positions easily. However, the hard skills can help these applicants to be more successful to win any kinds of these positions when they own these hard skills, e.g. microsoft offic, powerpoint, excel , word, microsoft project etc. softwares.

In conclusion, the global economy is dynamic and many of the skills required for positons in the future will need good technologies and work practices to be developed. The number of skills required t be successful in the jobs forecast to be most in demand in the future is growing. So, it explains that why future any one of these occupations which will need soft skills more than hard skills, due to organizations like to employ the employees who own managerial and analytical effort more than hard skills productive effort to assist their organizations to develop more easily.

Data -analysis skill needs

In the future, most organizations will have a number of jobs that include data analysis. Economists and labor market forecasters predict occupations need data analytical skill will need much. In addition, fast technological development means th types of technologies and applications workers in this field will need to be familiar with data analytical skill rapidly. It seems that data analytical jobs will have new job opportunity to employees with in-demand skills in future global labor market.

Why and how do employers demand for data analysis skills? Data analysis skills mean the ability to gather, analyze and draw practical conclusions from data as well as communicate data findings to others. The occupations include: data analyst, data scientist, statistician, market research analyst, financial analyst,research manager. In business career, many employers expect to employ statisticans, operations researh analysts, market research analysts and marketing specialists to assist their organizations to gather useful data from market in order to analyze and draw practical conclusions and finding the best solutions or methods to win their competitors.

Therefore, these data analysis jobs will have much need. Large size organizations with 500 or more employees were more likely than small or medium size organizations with 25 to 499 employees to plan hired data analysis positons in the future. For example, human source department will use big data to help make strategic decisions. How HR uses big data . HR will use big data for sourcing, recruitment, or selection, identifying causes of turnover and/or employee retention strategies or trends, managing talent and performance. Why organizations do not use big data. It is possible that they lack of knowledg expertise, the majority of organizatons will have data analysis positions within accounting and finance department, human resources department, business and administration department, information technology department, marketing, advertising and sales department, supply chain and operations department, research and development department, customer service department and other departments. So, future data analysis skill will need to used in different organizational departments.

However, publicly and privately owned for-profit organizations were more likely than government organizations to have data analysis positions in the marketing, advertising and sales function. Also, data analysis skills are required to different levels in any organizations , such as entry level, non-management / individual contributor level, mid-level management level, seniot management or executive level. The analyst, research analyst, market research analyst, scientist-based titles include: data scientists , research scientist, scientist, other descriptive titles include researcher, statistician, mathematician and other . So, data analysis positions will have many different skills to be selected to any one data analysis professional. For example, the data analysis professional can select either to learn the ability to interpret and communicate data analysis results skill or to learn how gathering or analyzing data skill. So, data analysis skill is not onlyone skill, it is more than one skill to let any one employee to select to learn.

Why do organizations need data analysis professionals? On workforce planning aspect, organizatons expect to let strategic direction and content of workforce needed for future business objectives easier, analyzing workforce: supply analysis, demand analsis and gap analysis more earier, developing action plan : recruiting and training plans to deal with gaps more easier, implementing action plan, monitoring, evaluating and revising plan more easier. So, organizations expect the data analysis professionsla can help them to solve these challenges, such as using of advanced technology solutons to integrate disparate planning sources; data availability and format; accessing to and understanding of the organization's data and analytics, developing business case to gain support from senior management and collaboration among HR staff, managers and executive easier. Future industries need data analysis professionals may include manufacturing health care and social assistance, scientific and technical service, finance and insurance, educational services , government agencies, retail trade, transportation and warehousing, construction, utilities, accomodation, and food services, waste management and remediation services, entetainment, and creation, real estate and rental and leasing , repair and maintenance, agriculture, forestry, fishing and hunting, personal and laundry services etc.

In conclusion, data analysis job need explains why future readiness and data analytical skills will be popular needed in globl labour market , due to these both skills are labour shortage and employers will need employees own big data readiness and data analytical both skills in order to win whose competitors more easier.

Q9 Why does future global skillful labor soft knowledge skill need increase ?

In the future several occupations have been identified as the most frequent movers between all labour market states. The elementary occupations include: waiters, bar staffs, clearners, catering assistants, construction and security service workers, care workers, sales assistants and general clerks etc. So, the low educational level workers can learn these soft wkills to raise whose professional workering level to prepare to do these above positions in global elementary occupation job market.

The changes of employer were most frequent for IT programmers, doctors, electricians, carpenters, skilled workers in global labour market. These skilled occupations will have manpower shortage supply challenge, due to either people feel the educatonal level is under low. So, there has no many people have interest to know these knowledg to prepare their elementary careers. So, these kinds of low skilled occupations will have not enough human power supply to global labour job market also, the high skilled or educational job support.

Moreover, the high skilled occupations also encounter labour shortage issue. The skills in short supply related to experienced canadidates e.g. five years or more. For example, pharmaceutical , biogharma and food innovation industries. The occupational shortage roles include: Chemists, analytical scientists, product formulation, analytical development for roles in biopharma, quality control analyst includes pharmaco-vigilance, i.e. drug safety roles. The demand for engineering industry aspect which will aos increase the labour shortage includes process and design (research and development, quality control, automation, lean processes) are skillful labours need to help employers to achieve these intentions. They may include raising competitiveness, boosting productivity and skills availability. So, if future these above any one of occupation labours can not achieve these benefits to satisfy their employers' needs. Then, his/her average weekly or hourly wages will be reduced. It means that the unskilled labour under skilled labour wage can not increased more easily, even they own many year working experiences in any one of above these occupations. If the employer feels the labour is unskilled or below skilled level for any one of these occupations in these any one industry aspect, e.g. wholesale and retal , human health, education, accomodaton and food , construction, professional activities, financial service , public administration, and defence, transportation etc. occupations. Then, these industries' unskilled or below skilled level workers' salaries will be lower level to compare the higher skilled workers who work in any one of these industries.

The reason why future employers need to employ skilled labours. One explanation for slow recovery in demand in negative impact on investment is a prolonged period of high unemployment. This is led to job weekers left labour market or became unemployable due. So, future low skillful level will be one important factor to cause unemployment in society as well as nowadays labours ought need consider whether their skills are needed to improve in order to avoid future competition in job market.